Writing:
The Hobby That Pays

Writing: The Hobby That Pays

by

Gordon Wells

RIGHT WAY
plus

Contents

Chapter 1:

Introduction

If you want to indulge in most hobbies, you have to pay for the privilege. Writing is different. Writing is a hobby that, if you are successful, pays you.

It's a great hobby. It allows you to communicate; it allows you to be creative. Initially, you may sell only the occasional piece of work; at first, you may be paid little. If you work at writing though – and if you have enough talent – you will do better. You will sell more and more of your work; you may sometimes get paid a lot!

Your hobby can become your full-time profession. Few are that successful though, so don't give up the day job yet.

Another plus point: you are never too old and, within reason, seldom too young to take up writing as a hobby. Most teenage magazines encourage readers to write to them; some pay for such contributions. And many a steamy best-selling romance has been written by a 70-year-old.

As a hobby, writing helps the young to grow up, to become mature; it helps older people to stay young at heart. A writer becomes more interested than his or her peers in everything that is going on around; this makes the writer a more rounded, more interesting person.

Basic equipment

What do you need in order to start as a writer? To start in a very small way you need no more than just pen and paper. We will see, in the next chapter, how you can make a start with no more equipment than that, writing letters. And sometimes

9

you will get paid for these letters. But nowadays, if you are going to make any sort of a show at your writing hobby, you will need a computer and a printer. You just cannot submit handwritten work to professional magazine editors; if you do, it is likely to be consigned straight to the waste basket – rejected.

Apart from the computer, you just need paper and ideas. You can build up your personal reference library as you go along.

Qualifications

You need no formal qualifications to become a writer. If your work is good and appropriately aimed, with a bit of luck, it will sell. If it's not, it won't. It's as simple as that.

Of course, if you want to write medical advice the editor will expect you to be a doctor – or perhaps a nurse. If you want to write about bringing up a baby, you won't have much success if you are an elderly bachelor. Unless . . .

If you want to write a book about writing, such as this one, you will need to convince the publisher that you know what you are talking about. I did. I do. I started writing many years ago, as a hobby, and 'learned the trade' in my spare time. I have no university degree in English Language nor in English Literature. In fact, I trained as a civil engineer, but I've always liked stringing words together. In my time I've written articles about Borneo (where I worked for a while), about statues of astronauts in Russia and Pharaohs in Egypt (both of these articles were based on everyday package-holiday experiences), about how to write letters and how to use the telephone, about the 'history' of dragons (one of my favourite subjects), about collecting Chinese jade and on the significance of Hallowe'en. I've written about so many different subjects that I've forgotten many of them.

The reason for listing some of the subjects I've written about is not to show how clever I am; it is to illustrate the breadth of subjects available to just one ordinary person. You can write – and sell – articles about almost anything. The knack (the skill) is to find out which magazines want which material. We'll look at the task of researching markets in Chapter 5.

So what then does it take to become a writer? You need:

- Enthusiasm – you must want to write (and to keep on writing, not just to have written).
- Dedication – the willingness to work at it (at the expense of other interests perhaps – you must make time).
- Resilience – the willingness to keep trying, despite the almost inevitable early failures.
- Interest – you must have, or develop, an interest in things and activities all about you, in people and their emotions, feelings and motivations – and you must wish to communicate that interest, to enthuse others.
- A love of words – a delight in stringing words together in what you believe is the most effective manner.

I believe that with no more than the above qualities anyone can become a writer. Maybe not a very successful writer, but at least one who gets the occasional piece of work published. To be really successful, talent is also necessary. But talent alone is not enough. Even with talent, the above qualities are still necessary. And a bit of luck will always come in handy.

Enthusiasm

Too many people want to be writers. They cherish the concept of being known as a writer. It is the kudos they crave rather than the ability to communicate. Such people give up when they discover how much hard work there is in writing. Which leads us nicely on to . . .

Dedication

Your writing is something that has to be fitted in, within your limited spare time. You will never learn to be a successful writer if you don't put the time in. Too many would-be writers complain that they don't have enough time. It becomes the excuse for their lack of achievement. The ones who become successful are those who make time for their writing.

You may have to get up early each morning to write (for an hour, say) before going off to work, or before the rest of the family wake. Maybe you'll have to sacrifice an hour of television time each night – as I did. Or work into the small hours. However you do it, make time you must. And you must persuade your family to accept this daily commitment of yours.

To become a writer you should work at it daily. It is no good sitting around waiting for the muse to alight on your shoulder and for those best-selling words to pour out effortlessly. The muse will only visit those who are ready for work; the result will only be good if you have learned your craft. The successful writer is the one who commands the muse to arrive at start-of-work time.

Resilience

The corollary of dedication is resilience. Few would-be writers are immediately successful. Some of us learn by our mistakes – it's a tough but effective school. If you want to be a successful writer, be prepared for your early work to be rejected.

Rejections hurt. There's no getting away from it, they really hurt. What makes it worse in the writing business is that you are seldom given a reason for a rejection. All you get is a printed rejection slip – sometimes nothing at all.

The only consolation that can be offered to the beginning writer is that we've all had rejections. And most writers, no matter how experienced, still suffer occasional rejections. They don't hurt any the less no matter how experienced you might be. But the successful writer shrugs his or her shoulders, checks through the rejected work to see if it really was no good – and why – and then gets on with the next piece of work.

Don't be put off by initial failure. Keep at it. Learn from your failures and you will improve. You will achieve success.

Interest

To be a successful writer, you must be interested in what you are writing about. If you are bored by your subject, how can you expect to interest the reader? And if you have but few interests, you will have only a few things to write about.

If you are trying to write non-fiction – feature articles or, eventually, books – you need a constant stream of ideas to write about. And they must be interesting ideas. It is your job, as a writer, to make dull facts interesting, stimulating, even amusing, to the previously uninterested reader.

If it's fiction you want to write, you must be interested in people: what makes them 'tick', what they are really feeling deep down, and what makes them do what they do. That is what readers want to read; they want to be able to identify with your characters, they want the characters to come alive. You can only give your readers what they want from your own prior interest in people.

A love of words

All the qualities outlined so far are of no use if you do not enjoy stringing words together. A writer is a wordsmith, a worker with words. You must work hard at identifying the right word – the *mot juste*.

You must work at your word-crafting to make your writing easy to understand. A good writer leaves academic texts to the academics; a good writer does not strive to impress the reader with his or her skill or learning; a good writer communicates – no more, no less.

Organizing yourself

I have already mentioned the need to make time for your writing. And I have mentioned the minimal expense and limited equipment that is necessary in order to make a start. But you do need a writing *place*.

Yes, of course you can write on the dining table or even, as one person I was told of, sitting in the (empty) bath. The place, as such, is unimportant. What is important is that your papers are secure. You need somewhere to keep them, away from prying eyes, away from children's jammy fingers – and away from the bath-water. Not that there is necessarily anything secret about your writing, but until you achieve your first success, your writing ego will be fragile and easily dented. Your writing ego will still be fragile even when you are successful, but you'll have learned to hide your feelings. Right from the start, arrange for a box or cupboard or drawer that is yours alone, for your writing, and is not to be touched by anyone.

As you become more involved in your new hobby though, you will want a better place. You will need somewhere, a desk, a cubby-hole – even just a wide shelf – where you can safely leave your work from one writing session to the next. And you will accumulate reference books too; they need to be in their proper place, close to hand when you are writing.

What to write

You have already decided that you want to be a writer: if you hadn't, you probably wouldn't have picked up this book. But a writer of what? Maybe your ambition is to write a best-selling novel – or to write beautiful verse. Perhaps you sit and watch your nightly television sit-coms and soaps and feel sure you could write something better. And this is great. But don't make up your mind too quickly. Think about all the writing areas.

You could choose the area within which you will write from the following, inevitably incomplete, list:

● Letters to the editors – often for payment.
● Fillers – hints and tips for others, or amusing snippets.

- Feature articles – on a variety of topics.
- Short stories – which might include picture-story scripts (for comics).
- Jokes for comedians or short sketches for radio/TV series.
- Poems – 'serious' verse, or simply witty rhymes.
- Novels – 'straight' or genre, for adults or children.
- Non-fiction books – which, as we shall see, range widely.
- Plays – for the stage, for radio, for TV, or for film.

The detailed requirements of each of those writing areas will differ, but they all have much in common. We shall look at a number of different ones in subsequent chapters.

Money

Before you sit down and start on your writing apprenticeship, there is one further matter to think about. Money.

Are you starting along the road to becoming a successful writer with the intention of making money, or just of enjoying what you're doing? Only a few big-name writers make a fortune from writing. There are many hundreds who work full time at writing and make a reasonable, if not spectacular, living at it. There are thousands of writers though, writing feature articles, short stories, novels or non-fiction books on a part-time basis and supplementing their income very nicely. Your earnings will vary with your choice of writing area.

If you write feature articles, you could be paid as little as £30 per thousand words – or several hundred pounds a time. But suppose you were writing articles for a £500-a-time market. You'd need to research, write, and sell an article every ten days or so to earn a meagre £15,000 a year; articles that pay big money will entail a lot of research. You'd have to work hard – full time – to sell two or three a month.

If you write for the more ordinary '£30–50 a thousand' markets, you'd need to sell a couple of articles every day to make the same income. That's almost impossible to achieve.

If you write short stories, you could be paid between £100 and £500 a story. Again, that's one every two or three days at the bottom end of the market or every week-and-a-half at the upper end. Neither would be easy. (And the market for short stories is in decline and anyway much smaller than that for articles.)

But what you really want to do is write a novel, isn't it? Ideally, 'The Great British Novel'. A first novel, maybe 60,000 to 100,000 words long, might attract an initial payment of around £3,000. If you were really lucky this first novel might be published in both hardback and paperback. OK, maybe £5,000. If it took you less than a year to write this first novel in your 'spare time', you'd be most unusual.

Of course, with the right novel, there are possibilities for all sorts of spin-off earnings. You might sell film/TV rights, etc., or hit the jackpot with your paperback sales. But few first novels (or second, third or fourth novels) achieve such success.

The earnings from novels vary too with the type of story. The biggest-earning novels are usually those in the genre categories – romances, whodunits, science-fiction stories, etc.; few writers earn much from the straight, more 'literary' novel, which is much harder to sell.

You would have more likelihood of selling a non-fiction book; many more non-fiction books than novels are published. But while non-fiction books often earn more than run-of-the-mill first novels, there is no jackpot to dream of. They seldom make films from instructional books.

Many people, about to retire, dream of writing their autobiography. ('I've had such an interesting life.') There is not a large market for the memoirs of 'ordinary' people though, only for declining media stars or significant achievers.

If you must, it is better to think of writing your autobiography as a historic record for the family, a labour of love without hope of financial reward. Indeed, to record the story of your life is a marvellous thing to do: you will have all the pleasure of writing it, and in many years' time, its portrayal of everyday life in bygone days will fascinate one of your descendants. Just don't expect to get it published.

And if you want to write poetry, don't think of making any money at it. Many poets end up paying for their work to be printed.

Although this book is about writing as a hobby that pays, it is now possible and practical to print a few dozen copies of a book very cheaply, using a commercial 'short-run' book printer. If you just want fewer than 100 copies for family and friends, this can be done economically.

Self-publishing

Self-publishing is an increasingly available option for writers unable to get their work into print in any other way. It is perhaps a reasonable proposition for some types of work:

- For poetry – for which it is almost (but not quite) impossible to find a commercial publisher. Poets can often sell their self-published books when reading their work for an audience.
- For local history books – the history of a village, or small geographical area. Mainstream publishers will seldom be interested in publishing for such a limited readership-population – but such books can often readily be sold in local shops.
- For very specialised non-fiction subjects where there is, again, a limited and specialist market which the writer is familiar with.

It is very seldom a suitable road for a novelist to go down.

Self-publishing entails the writer becoming involved in all the non-writing processes of publishing . . . and marketing. It also entails the writer in paying for the book to be produced – hoping that the investment will be recouped. And that is outside the scope of this book.

No. Think of writing, as the title says, as a paying hobby. It won't cost you much, but few of us earn real riches either. You will, though, derive immense pleasure and satisfaction every time something you have written is published. No matter how small it is, you will have created it, out of your own head. It's a great hobby.

Chapter 2:

Getting Started

Just about anyone can write – something. Maybe you'll never become a best-selling novelist, a newspaper columnist or a TV script-writer. But if you can write a chatty letter or talk interestingly to a friend, then you can become a published writer.

Get into print

Every beginning writer needs the encouragement of seeing his or her work in (paid) print as soon as possible. Let me show you one way to achieve this.

Most of the more popular magazines feature 'Letters to the Editor' columns. Many pay for each letter they publish. Some offer prizes or bigger payments for the 'Letter of the Week/Month'. The magazines are eager to receive letters from their readers and will pay for them. If you can write an appropriate letter you could achieve your first paid publication.

Don't scoff at this suggestion. Many experienced writers continue to submit 'Letters to the Editor' long after they achieve success with more sophisticated written work; they often earn enough to cover a year's postal expenses on their 'real' writing – or a weekend break. And letters don't take long to write.

Writing a 'Letter to the Editor' is also good basic training for the beginning writer. Before attempting to write such a letter, you must do some market research. You need to:

●   Find out which magazines invite letters from readers.

- Choose one or two 'target magazines' to 'attack', (select the magazines which use the largest number of letters per issue, thereby offering you the greatest chance of success).
- Check that they pay for all letters published, not just the 'star' letter.
- Read the published letters in two or three issues.
- Identify the favourite subjects and the type of letter – serious or witty, anecdotal or hard factual.
- Check on the usual length of letters.

The basic rule

You will probably find that the most popular letters are personalised, anecdotal, and slightly amusing. Almost certainly the letters will be short, seldom more than 200 words. So now you know the sort of letter the magazine's editor likes to publish.

Not only that, but you will have seen how much is paid. Many UK magazines pay at least £5 per published letter; and letters are often no more than 100 words long. Convert that to a rate per 1,000 words and 'Letters' suddenly become respectable . . . earning £50+ per 1,000 words.

The basic rule that all writers – not just Letter-writers – must learn is:

Give the editor what he/she wants.

You're in a buyer's market. The editor is always right. As a writer seeking publication – and payment – it is no good thinking that you can change editorial policy. Every editor knows (or, at least, thinks he knows) just what the magazine's readers want.

If the 'Letters' page has short, witty, personalised letters, that's what you must send the editor. Don't try to buck the system. It will serve no purpose at all to write a vitriolic condemnation of present-day morals or about the failings of modern medicines. Your letter will go straight to the waste-bin. You will have wasted your time. And, more important, the editor's, which is a far more heinous crime.

Which magazine?

The more thoroughly you know your 'target' magazine the better. The more you are 'at one' with their typical readers, the more readily can you write what they want to read.

You may have in mind an amusing, highly publishable letter about a motoring experience. You would reduce your chances of acceptance and publication if you sent this letter to the editor of a mass-market women's magazine. It would have a better chance of success in a motoring or popular 'family' publication. Similarly, a letter about how your baby sister (or grandchild) was potty-trained, would stand its best chance in a young mothers' magazine.

Many hobby and craft magazines – DIY, gardening, photography, etc. – invite and pay for letters. Some letter topics could be equally appropriate for a general-interest readership as for a specialist one. You should think hard about which magazine would be the most suitable for your letter. The possible payment for each letter would undoubtedly have a bearing on which you choose. Many magazines require that an offered letter should not previously have been published.

You will find out which magazine to submit which letter to by studying the published letters; and then you can write something similar. Don't copy, don't write about a too-similar experience, activity or observation, but don't be too different either. Just along the same lines.

Letter subjects

What is your first letter going to be about? Ideas are everywhere. Think about your day, think about your journey to work. Think of what made you smile, what made you happy, or proud, or sad. Think *amusing*. Think *interesting*.

To illustrate the many things that 'Letters' can be written about, consider these:

- The 'star' letter in a do-it-yourself magazine was from a wife telling how she had bought her husband a home-assembly desk for his birthday. Wisely, she left him alone to assemble it. Later, having heard appropriate sounds from the 'assembly-room', she went back, expecting to see the desk. She was disappointed. It had taken all that time to extract the desk pieces from the packing, and he hadn't even finished doing that. This letter was just under 120 words long. It won a prize valued at £50.

- A secondary schoolgirl wrote to a women's magazine about her Saturday job in a small shop. In the shop, she had had to learn to add simple figures in her head – without a calculator. She wondered why she had not been taught such useful skills in maths at school, instead of complicated but less relevant algebra. This letter consisted of three paragraphs, the whole just over 100 words.
- A grandmother wrote to another popular women's magazine about her grandson. Fascinated by dinosaurs, he was looking at pictures of them in a book. One dinosaur had the word 'Rex' in its name and he wondered why. He thought for a few moments. Then, 'Probably because it wrecks everything,' he declared. Only 50 words, but it earned a fiver: a rate of £100 a thousand words.
- A women's magazine carried a letter from a man. He had been having coffee with his wife in a local café and had carelessly knocked over his full cup. A young waitress cheerfully cleared up the mess. Walking away, she had glanced back to smile reassuringly at the couple and crashed into a post, dropping a trayful of crockery.

All these examples have important features in common. They are all about ordinary, everyday, personal experiences. They nearly all make the reader smile. They are short, sharp and to the point: there is no padding, no waffle, just a concise anecdote.

What made you smile?

Think carefully about what you have seen or done over the last few days. Chances are that some incident made you smile, or wonder. You could write a 'Letter' about that.

A letter arrived by post the other day. When I opened the envelope, it was empty. What had I missed? Why should anyone post me an empty envelope? Where had the intended contents gone? I shall write a 'Letter' about that incident one day.

I 'lost' my car in a helical multi-storey car park some while ago. I had made a note of the bay in which I parked it – but it wasn't there when I returned. Plodding disconsolately down the ramp, to report the loss to the police, I noticed that the parking bay numbers that I was passing were all coloured blue. But surely, when I parked, the bay number had been in red? Then it dawned on me. The car park consisted of two interwoven spirals numbered in red and blue . . . and I was on the 'wrong' spiral. I'm definitely going to write a 'Letter' about that.

Writing the letter

So you know the sort of letter that your 'target' magazine prefers. You have an idea for a suitable letter. What next?

Now you've got to write it. Write it simple. Don't write to impress anyone. Just imagine you're telling your spouse, or mum, or work-colleague about it. Don't waste anyone's time with a lengthy introduction or explanation; jump straight in with the real point of the story. (It doesn't matter why I was in that car park. It doesn't matter who sent me the empty envelope. The reader wants the story, not the background.)

Once you've written your letter-story, rewrite it. Go through it carefully. Cross out all the unnecessary words, delete the repetitions, remove all the 'I thoughts' and all the 'verys'. Now count the number of words in your letter-story. If there are more than 200, it's too long: probably too much explanation.

Keep deleting words and phrases until you've got it down to an absolute minimum. Check too that your sentences are not over-long. Short sentences are always better. (See the next chapter for more detailed advice on writing style.) Read it through, aloud, listening for phrases that 'don't sound right'.

Now type or write your letter out neatly – it doesn't have to be typed. It's a *reader's* letter, not a writer's.

Despatching the letter

Pop your letter in an envelope and post it off. (Some magazines welcome emailed letters nowadays – and that's even better, it saves you the postage.) Keep a copy – you've done a lot of work on it – and make a note of the date you posted it. Now forget it. You can't write a similar letter about the same incident to another magazine for several months; you must wait to see if it is used, and to get paid. The magazine won't tell you whether it is going to be used. It'll just appear or go into the waste-bin. If it hasn't appeared in the magazine in, say, six months, try sending another copy to a different magazine.

Conflicting directly with the advice about submitting your writing work that is given in later chapters of this book, when sending in 'Letters':

- Don't try to look professional.
- Don't enclose a stamped addressed envelope.
- Don't ask for an unused letter to be returned.
- Don't use a (writing) business letter-heading.
- Don't tell the editor how you wish to be paid.
- Don't ask for a free copy of the issue in which it is published (you're supposed to be a regular reader).

Not all of your 'Letters to the Editor' will be published. But if you keep trying, you'll soon get one published. Once that's happened – you're a writer. Keep writing these short letters to magazines. In time, you'll get more expert at it and will be able to write them more quickly. It's a good sideline.

And if the letters are frequent, knowledgeable, reader-helpful, and to any sort of specialist magazine, the editor may begin to notice your name. Maybe then, you can offer the magazine a feature article – see Chapter 6.

Hints, tips and fillers

Some magazines also welcome readers' hints and tips. Again, you must study your own markets to determine which magazines welcome them. They will often use them in a special page or column of hints. The submission requirements for such hints will usually be somewhere on the same page. If the magazine says hints should be typed, type them; if they ask for them one per sheet of paper, give them one hint per sheet; if they require the enclosure of a voucher from the magazine, enclose one.

Letters are not the only short written snippets that you can sell to magazines. Some magazines also welcome *fillers*. (They may not say so – observe for yourself. It's called market research.) Fillers are just that: something to fill up an incomplete column of text. Look at most magazines and newspapers: you will often see short, less-than-200-word, self-contained items at the end of longer articles and news stories.

(*Reader's Digest* is one of the best-known markets in the world for fillers; and they pay very well indeed for them. But because they pay well, it's a difficult market to break into. Don't tackle it until you are an experienced filler-writer. Serve your apprenticeship on lesser magazines.)

Fillers are often short factual pieces. The more interesting or surprising the facts, the better the chance of selling the filler.

In the absence of specific advice on how to submit hints, tips and fillers, I suggest you write them up as concisely as possible and submit them, typed double-spaced, one per sheet of A4 paper. They need to be every bit as crisp and tightly-written as your 'Letters'. Many hints and tips are no more than 50-word items.

If I could, I would submit perhaps half a dozen such snippets at a time. Make sure that you give your name and address on each sheet containing hint, tip or filler. You can also, usually, be somewhat more professional when submitting fillers. (With 'Readers' Hints' though, it may well be best to submit as for a 'Letter'. Use your own judgement.)

That's it. Amaze yourself. Impress your friends. Get into print. Become a writer. Write your first – paid – 'Letter'. Now.

Chapter 3:

An Effective Writing Style

Don't be put off by the title of this chapter. For your writing hobby to be successful, you don't need a degree in English Literature. You just need to write so that those who read it can easily understand it.

Always remember that writing is a communication process: a means of passing on your advice, your knowledge, your thoughts and ideas, your stories to others. For the communication to be complete you need a reader – and the reader must 'get the message'. If you write in a high-falutin way there's a good chance that readers won't understand what you're trying to say. And bored, puzzled readers quickly switch off and stop reading.

Now that we've all left school there are no captive readers. You, the writer, have to capture, and then retain, the reader's interest. What you write has to be 'a good read'.

The basic principles of effective writing

There are good reasons for the continuing popularity of J. K. Rowling's *Harry Potter* novels, of Keith Waterhouse's newspaper columns, of Alan Ayckbourn's plays; they all write to interest their readers, their audience, in a style that is easily understood.

Already then, we can spell out the first basic principle of effective writing:

1. Write for your reader – not for yourself.

And the first principle leads us directly on to the second. What does the reader want?

The reader simply wants to take in the story, the message, the advice that you are striving to convey. The reader does not want to have to interpret your words before taking them in: we're all supposed to be using a common language. The reader doesn't want to have to think what you're saying, what you are getting at; he or she wants to understand straight away. Think how easily you and your neighbour chat over the garden fence; if you each couldn't understand what the other was going on about, you'd soon say so or stop chatting.

From the foregoing, the second basic principle of effective writing is already clear:

2. Write clearly – for easy understanding.

We'll come back to the details of how to write clearly; for the moment let's extend our look at your chatty neighbour. If he or she talks 'over your head', ignoring your signals that he has 'lost you', then he is no longer communicating. Your neighbour is then – even if unintentionally – merely showing off; seeking to impress you with his or her greater knowledge or skill. And nobody likes a 'show-off'.

Similarly, the last thing a reader wants is a reminder of how clever you are, what a 'good writer' you are. Certainly at the popular level, the less the writer intrudes into the communication process the better.

Hence, the third basic principle, which is really just a restatement of the first two:

3. Never seek to impress the reader with your own cleverness or skill.

Really, the more transparent – unnoticeable – the writer can become, the better the reader will absorb the story, the advice or the information. It's the message that's important, not how it's transmitted.

But transparency alone is not enough. The reader must be interested – all the time. And that gives us our fourth, and final, basic principle:

4. Capture the reader's interest quickly – and retain it.

As mentioned at the start of this chapter, now that we've all left school, there is no captive market. No teacher to say, 'Read that'. You've got to make the reader *want* to read what you write. That's what effective writing is all about.

Addressing your reader

If you are writing a letter to your grandchild you would write more simply than if writing to an elderly college professor. By considering such extremes, the need to write for the reader is obvious. The interests, and ability to understand, of 25-year-old women differ from those of 45-year-olds too. Nor will the interests and priorities of a young mother with a part-time factory job have much in common with someone from the London 'jet set'.

The other side of the same coin is your own knowledge and enthusiasm. The person reading your article on carriage clocks may not have your background knowledge, nor your interest. The writer's job is to lead the readers along easily and to enthuse them. And don't assume that the readers will be as interested as you in all the fascinating details of 'the widget that fits onto the third sproggle at the back of the gizmo'. They aren't.

To pitch your writing at the right level of knowledge and interest, you need to know just who your typical average reader is. Initially, writing for magazines that you read and know well, it will be safe to assume that your reader is someone much like yourself. Soon though, you will need to find out more about the readers of other magazines for which you are writing. Chapter 5 looks at this market research in detail.

Writing clearly

Think again of the neighbourly chats already mentioned. Both you and your neighbour talk easily – as long as there

are no attempts at 'one-upmanship' – clearly and understand-
ably to each other. This is 'the norm'.

Put a piece of paper in front of many people though, and a
pen in their hands, and they want to use different words.
Longer words, 'impressive' words, fine-sounding words. The
fluency of their spoken words is lost. Too many people treat
written English as a different language from spoken English.
It should not be.

An American management and communication *guru*, Robert Gunning, succinctly advises his clients to 'write as you
talk'. Recalling the hesitation, the repetitions, the poor gram-
mar and the faulty sentence structure of many people's speech
though, I would amend that advice to 'write as you would like
to talk'. But we'll come back to the uses of the spoken word in
writing later.

Your reader wants your writing to be clear. How can you
best achieve this?

For writing to be clear, it needs to be simple. By definition,
complicated writing is not easy to understand; simple writing
is.

Simple writing usually comes from brevity. Short words are
easy to understand, a short sentence is seldom difficult to
understand, a short paragraph at least *looks* easy to absorb.
And, overall, the smoother your writing flows, the easier it is
to read.

Short, simple words

Consider, next, your own reading experience. Every now and
then all of us come across a word we don't understand. Our
immediate reaction is to assume that the meaning will soon
become clear from its context. If it doesn't, and if we are
sitting comfortably at home, and because we writers actively
enjoy words, we may consult the dictionary. (Many readers
will not.) If we ourselves are reading the magazine on holiday,
or on a train journey, it could well be inconvenient to consult
a dictionary. We ignore the incomprehensible word and read
on.

Given two or three such words in a single feature article or short story, many readers will just give up. Ordinary magazines are not in the business of educating their readers in the finer points of an English vocabulary.

The moral is that, as writers, we should use simple words. Generally speaking, short words are easily understood; long words are more likely to be unfamiliar (and less likely to be used in everyday speech).

The first rule of thumb then for clear writing is:

Use short words – preferably of no more than three basic syllables. Prefer words with which most people are familiar. If you have to use a long/difficult word though, so be it; but try to ensure that its meaning is made clear by its context.

Short, simple sentences

Think now about sentences. We were taught at school that a sentence should have a subject, an object and a verb. With a short sentence, this is easy. In long sentences though, it is all too easy to get lost in the grammatical construction and omit one or other of the essentials. In a long sentence, with the inevitable clauses and qualifications of the basic thought, the logic too can readily become confused.

That is not to say that a long sentence is necessarily bad. The masters of English literature have often used long sentences to great effect. But it requires careful thought to produce a good, long sentence. By comparison, it is relatively easy to write a good, clear, short sentence. It is even easier, though, to write a poor, difficult-to-understand, long sentence.

Many people write over-long sentences almost without thinking. It is a common fault.

Look at some of your own past writings. Count the words in the sentences. Notice how many sentences are made up of 20, 30, even 40 words. Take one of your long sentences and consider whether it might not have been better as two or more shorter sentences. Look for an 'and' somewhere near the middle. Often, the 'and' can be replaced by a full-stop and a subsequent capital letter. Ask yourself whether the qualifying clause in mid-sentence might not have been better as a separate sentence in its own right.

Count the words

Now review the sentences in a published feature article or short story of the kind you aspire to write. In most popular magazines you will find that the *average* sentence length is around 15 or 16 words. Seldom will you find a sentence longer than 25 words.

For this purpose, when counting sentence lengths, treat semi-colons and colons as though they were full-stops. Except where the colon introduces a list, the semi-colon and colon serve much the same purpose as a full-stop. The phrases on either side of the semi-colon and colon are often complete in their own right. The linking by punctuation emphasizes the association of ideas.

Aim at a fairly short average sentence length. This will undoubtedly improve your writing.

So, to put figures to this, the second rule of thumb for clear writing is:

Aim at an average sentence length of 15 words and an absolute maximum of 25 words. For counting purposes, treat semi-colons and colons as full-stops. (And remember that each 25-word sentence needs a 5-word one to maintain the average.)

And an important qualification: all short sentences or all average-length sentences can be dull – or staccato and 'jumpy' – so always vary your sentence lengths around the average. (Unless you specifically want to create an urgency with short sentences or a feeling of tranquillity with a sequence of long ones.)

When your confidence and writing skills are more developed, ignore this rule if you wish. I still work to it, more or less. Count my words.

Simple punctuation

If you will follow the above rule and use short sentences, it is barely necessary to talk about the need for simple punctuation. Short sentences need no more than full-stops and commas.

Until you feel fully confident in your writing style, there is also much to be said for not using semi-colons or colons at all (save in a list). As already mentioned, they are virtually interchangeable with a full-stop. And full-stops are certainly easier to use.

The third rule of thumb for clear writing is, therefore, as already stated:

Use simple punctuation – prefer full-stops and commas only.

The only punctuation marks requiring further comment are the exclamation mark and the dash.

The exclamation mark should seldom be used. It is too often the fall-back recipe of an ineffective writer seeking to show the emphasis that should have been conveyed by the words themselves. The exclamation mark, together with underlining and the use of coloured inks, is the hallmark of 'Disgusted, Tunbridge Wells'. Leave it to them.

(Of course, the exclamation mark has its occasional place in dialogue. Otherwise, the effective writer should use it about once every other month.)

The dash is often used in pairs, and is then a substitute for brackets; it is also sometimes used in lieu of a colon, linking two associated thoughts. It is a rather informal punctuation mark; I use it too often, for which I am often criticized. (By book editors, but seldom by magazine editors.) Informality is no bad thing. Remember, *write as you talk*, but avoid overdoing it.

Short paragraphs

You are strongly advised to write in short paragraphs – but not just for reasons of clarity or simplicity. Short paragraphs look better.

Think of those age-old newspapers that we sometimes see reproduced today. Note the overall grey appearance of the pages. This greyness is a product of:

- No pictures.
- No banner headlines.
- Long paragraphs – leaving a minimum of blank 'white space' around them.

The overall impression is one of unalleviated text. Boring.

Look now at the paragraphs in books and modern newspapers. You may find a few over-long paragraphs in learned textbooks and the more staid of the 'quality' newspapers. They look as though they are going to be heavy reading – and often are. Particularly in the more popular newspapers and in books like this, though, paragraphs will be fairly short: the paragraph indents and the end-of-line blank spaces give an impression of spaciousness and easy readability. Short paragraphs *look* easy to read.

However, 'short' is not, in this case, a specific measure. A 100-word paragraph in a narrow newspaper column might look quite long; the same paragraph in a typical book's 10cm page-width would not. To best judge a suitable average paragraph length, you need to think where it is to be used.

For most magazines a general guide can be suggested for a fourth rule of thumb – not so much for clear writing as for the appearance of easy readability:

> *For magazine publication, write to an average paragraph length of about 60 words and a maximum of about 100 words. (For books you can, if you wish, increase both figures by 20 to 30 words.) But again, and a big but: a sequence of same-length paragraphs can look very dull; so always vary the lengths of paragraphs.*

There is a further consideration affecting the length of paragraphs: a paragraph should deal with no more than one basic concept – a unit of thought, as Fowler's *Modern English Usage* has it. A paragraph 'must be homogenous in subject-matter . . .'

Fowler goes on to recommend that if a single unit of thought would make too long a paragraph, then that unit may be divided into more than one paragraph. Two separate units of thought, however, may not be combined to make a 'good-looking' single paragraph: this would destroy the essential unity of thought.

Another good reason for keeping your paragraphs short.

An easy read

So far, all the advice on writing style has been almost mechanistic. Apart from these rules of thumb there are other ways to make your writing read easily.

I have already commended the use of short, simple words; this advice can be extended to recommend the use of everyday words. Don't be afraid of writing in colloquial English. Don't be afraid of breaking some of the 'rules' that teacher hammered home at school.

Two important school-day rules that can sometimes be broken, or at least bent, are:

- **You may not start a sentence with 'and' or 'but'.**
  Oh yes, you may. If you use these words too often at the start of your sentences the whole will read badly. But doing it occasionally makes your writing come alive. And, as explained below, these little words help to smooth the *flow* of your writing.
- **You should not abbreviate the word 'not' (as in don't, etc.).**
  Yes, you may. Again, though, don't do it too often. (It can also be quite useful to use the 'more correct' form when you wish to emphasize something: e.g., 'Do not . . .' seems a more positive prohibition than a mere 'Don't . . .')

To be an 'easy read', your writing must *flow* freely. Some of my earlier recommendations may hinder the smoothness of flow though. Short sentences are, by their nature, jumpy: more akin to a staircase than a free-flowing stream. Short paragraphs, particularly those where the single unit of thought is incomplete, are also sometimes a hindrance to smooth flow.

Improve the flow

The skilful writer smoothes out the wordy peaks and troughs and improves the flow by:

- Avoiding a string of disjointed and 'jumpy' short sentences and varying the sentence lengths.
- Easing the jump from one paragraph to the next (between sentences too) by using link-words and phrases.

Paragraph links remind the reader of where he/she has come from; how the ensuing paragraph elaborates on the thoughts of the previous one. Useful link-words and phrases include:

> There are other ways ...
> Similarly ...
> That was not the only ...
> Not only does ... but ...
> Therefore ...
> It follows that ...
> After that ...

And then there are those two little words already mentioned, ideal for linking sentences and paragraphs:

> But then ...
> But that may never happen.
> And, of course, there is also ...
> And ...

Having added in these link-words and phrases while drafting, you may later decide to remove them at the 'polishing' stage (see below). This does not matter. Even if you do decide to 'polish them out', they will have served their purpose: they will have made you think about the flow. (My first draft of this paragraph started with 'And'. I deleted it while polishing.)

Seize the reader's interest

No matter how well your writing flows, and how easy a read your work is, it must also be of interest. In a story, something has to be happening; a feature article must be chock-full of useful information. As I have already said: there are no more captive readers. Whatever you are writing, you must seize the reader's attention quickly. And then keep a firm grip on it.

Observe a casual shopper browsing through the racks of magazines: the pages are turned, pictures are glanced at, a few titles are noticed. If a story or feature title attracts attention, or if the related illustration is sufficiently eye-catching, the first paragraph of actual text may be read. If that opening paragraph is interesting, the magazine may be bought and the story or feature read. If not, it stays on the shelf.

Much the same process goes on even when a magazine has been bought and the reader is deciding what to read within it. There is no one around to tell the reader that 'this piece gets better as you get into it'.

Similarly, books are often bought/borrowed/read on the strength of the cover picture, the back-cover 'blurb', any inside pictures and – if you're lucky – the first page.

You have to seize the reader's interest in the first one or two paragraphs of a short story or feature article and the first 250–300 words of a book. These first few words are known as 'the hook'. In many ways, they are the most important words in the whole article/story/book.

The opening paragraph of a feature article will form a more effective hook if it is shorter than average. If you are writing to an average paragraph length of 60 words, make the opening paragraph half that, just 30 words. A short paragraph made up of short sentences is easy to read – a better hook. In a short story, 'active' dialogue often makes a good hook.

But it is not enough that the reader's interest has been hooked: it then has to be held. To ensure this, articles should be 'structured' and stories should 'move'.

Think about the facts, activities or emotions you are going to describe. List them, perhaps. Ponder on the sequence of their presentation.

Whether in fiction or non-fiction, you may wish to report events in a straightforward chronological sequence; alternatively, you can start later and then fill in the earlier details in a 'flashback'. In a straight, factual article it may merely be a matter of arranging the facts in an interesting and logical order.

Whichever approach you adopt, you need to start with a bang, provide the reader with lesser explosions (of varying loudness) along the way, and then end with . . . another bang. Try to get the reader personally involved right from the start: then maintain this involvement throughout.

Now polish

By following the advice in this and later chapters, and by knuckling down to the actual writing, you will soon find that you have written a short story, a feature article, or a chapter of your book. You may think that's it. You're wrong. Now comes the really hard work: the polishing.

Ideally, put aside whatever you have written for a few days. The aim is to come back to your work able to review it as though it were written by someone else.

You will find it useful to read your work aloud. 'Aloud aloud', not just mouthing the words quietly to yourself. Read it aloud, so that you can hear the words coming back in, through your ears. The object is to involve a fresh sense in the reviewing process.

As you read through your work listen for the pomposities. We all tend, on occasion, to use unnecessarily long or unusual words and phrases just because they 'look good'. Identify these and delete them ruthlessly.

Does it sound right?

Listen for the phrases that don't sound quite right when you say them: the 'unspeakable English'. Change them. Before you stop, satisfy yourself that every phrase, every sentence, feels comfortable when spoken.

Identify too any sentence that gives you a warm feeling of literary pride as you read it. Once found . . . delete it and write it again, more simply.

Don't worry, we all over-write; the successful writers are the ones who discard their 'literary gems' – who 'murder their darlings'.

Read through again, silently now, looking for over-long sentences that have slipped in without your noticing. Eliminate the qualified superlatives and the like – the 'very excellents' and the 'slightly pregnants'. Shorten the sentences, remove all inappropriate qualifications. Look for vagueness and uncertainty: tighten up the facts. Are there any sentences you can phrase more clearly?

And cut out the unnecessary words. We all use too many. You should be able to delete at least one word in ten from a first draft. The word 'very' is (very) often a (very) good candidate for deletion: it adds (very) little. Tighten up your writing: make it crisper, less woolly, less waffly. It will be all the better for it.

Finally, re-read your tighter, waffle-free revision. Does it still flow smoothly? Or have you polished away all the links and all the individuality? If it no longer flows as well as it should, put back some 'smoothing' – but only enough to do the trick.

Chapter 4:

The Writing Content

So far we have talked about the way you 'join the words together', the somewhat mechanistic practice of concise simplicity. Let us now consider what to say.

The object of any writer is to communicate. To convey his or her ideas, feelings and enthusiasms to the reader. In fiction – short stories or novels – a large part of the writing process is to persuade the reader to identify with the fictional characters. (We shall look at characterisation in Chapter 9.) All forms of writing, though, need to be descriptive. Your reader must be able to visualise the scene.

Be descriptive

The scene you wish to describe may be your kitchen or garden, the setting for a light-hearted personal experience article; it may be a historic battlefield, the setting for a factual article about a famous person; or it may be the view from the heroine's bedroom window, providing essential background colour for a story. No matter what you are writing about, you have to describe it.

It pays to think of yourself, as a writer, as being in the entertainment business. That'll keep your feet on the ground. Few writers achieve the status of literary giants, to be studied by unwilling schoolchildren; most of us are well satisfied with providing a little light reading – entertainment, interest, or simple advice.

If your scene descriptions are too 'wordy', the ordinary reader will merely skip them.

Consider John Ruskin's nineteenth century description of a painting of Land's End by Turner:

> At the Land's End there is to be seen the entire disorder of the surges, when every one of them, divided and entangled among promontories as it rolls, and beaten back post by post from walls of rock on this side and that side, recoils like the defeated division of a great army, throwing all behind it into disorder, breaking up the succeeding waves into vertical ridges, which in their turn, yet more totally shattered upon the shore, retire in more hopeless confusion, until the whole surface of the sea becomes one dizzy whirl of rushing, writhing, tortured, undirected rage, bounding and crashing, myriads of waves, of which every one is not, be it remembered, a separate surge, but part and portion of a vast one, actuated by eternal power, and giving in every direction the mighty undulation of impetuous life, which glides over the rocks and writhes in the wind, overwhelming the one and piercing the other with the form, fury and swiftness of a sheet of lambent fire.

Phew! Apart from the fact that it is all in one sentence and therefore difficult to read, all Ruskin is saying is:

> The sea was very rough.

Ruskin got away with that descriptive passage in the nineteenth century. You and I could not get away with a similar passage today. Most editors would just reject any piece of work containing such a sentence/paragraph.

Of course, merely saying that the sea was rough would not suffice. The reader would not readily picture the scene without more guidance.

Without implying that my own writing is in any way comparable with Ruskin's, I might describe such a scene more briefly:

> Wave upon wave piled high, then crashed down in tumult. The sea grew even angrier. The mountains of water followed

each other ever faster, breaking on the rocks and writhing back in disarray. The very heavens disappeared in the all-pervading spray.

Even there I was beginning to get carried away with the sheer joy of choosing just the right words. (And note my 'different' use of 'very'.)

The rule for descriptive writing in the twenty-first century must be: be brief, be colourful – and use everyday words.

Paint word-pictures

Every beginning writer should practise descriptive writing. Try this exercise. Take a picture postcard of a view, or an advertising picture of a holiday location. Describe the scene, the whole scene, and nothing but the scene . . . and all in no more than, say, 200 words. Now go through what you have written and delete all the adjectives. Most beginners, when trying to be descriptive, use too many adjectives.

Now indulge yourself and put back one or two – no more – of the offending qualifiers. Your writing will be much stronger for this disciplinary exercise.

But a once-off exercise will not suffice. Many writers find it helpful to keep an 'everyday' or 'commonplace' book, a book in which they record all the little snippets they wish to preserve. When next you are impressed by a scene – a spectacular landscape or just the lived-in furnishings of a cosy room – write a description of it.

It will not always be possible for you to sit down there and then and paint a work-picture of a scene you wish to preserve. You may be passing through a strange town. You may not be able to stop. If possible, take a photograph of the scene: even if you are not a good photographer your 'happy snap' will suffice to remind you of the details. You can paint a convincing word-picture from even the worst, blurred, out-of-focus snap.

If it's not even possible to take a quick photograph, concentrate mentally for a few moments; capture the essentials and the overall 'feel'. If possible, make a few quick notes. Think of a word or two to describe the brightness of the colours, the stark simplicity of the chairs, the blackness of the gloom. Then write up your word-picture as soon as possible thereafter.

Don't restrict your word-pictures solely to scenes; practise describing people too. Describe their clothes, their hair, their appearance generally, the glint in their eye, the twisted smile, their mannerisms and their nervous movements. And, particularly if your ambition is to write fiction, extend your factual description by hypothesising on what the person does for a job, what they might be thinking, how they might react to various stimuli. In other words, exercise your imagination – start being creative.

Write for the senses

Too many beginning writers are unnecessarily restrictive in their descriptions. We each possess at least five senses. The successful writer plays on them all. Let your reader:

- **See** the extra-clear colour of the rain-soaked grass.
- **Hear** the music of the wind in the trees.
- **Smell** the warm breath of the lovely nut-brown horse as he takes the sugar-lump.
- **Feel** the harsh bark of the trees, the unevenness of the cobbles underfoot.
- **Taste** the spicy tang of some exotic food. Even **sense** the electric atmosphere, perhaps.

Grass is not just green, it can be emerald-green or maybe a parched greeny-brown. The wind needn't just whistle through the woods: sometimes it howls, or wanders silently, or barely rustles the dried leaves. Pop music may – to some people – thud, bludgeon and howl; classical music may caress (or stupefy) the senses. Food can have the unique spicy-hot smell of a curry; a flower the sickly-sweet fragrance of the frangipani. A man's fear may be recognisable by the acrid smell of stale sweat. Textures feel rough or smooth, coarse or silky, slippery or tweedy and can sometimes evoke extremely sensual reactions in the reader. And the tongue can experience a variety of flavours – the only problem is in adequately describing them. Put words to the various senses and the reader will more readily be 'in the picture'.

And see also the advice on 'show, don't tell' in Chapter 9.

The whole picture

If you are writing a novel, maybe your hero and heroine are sitting down to a meal. The discussion at the meal will be important, it will move the plot forward. (Dialogue is discussed in Chapter 9.)

But it is not enough merely to say that the two sat down for a meal. The reader will enter into the spirit of the scene better if the meal itself is described. (But probably not in a short story, there's not enough room.) The description should make the reader's mouth water.

> The avocado pear was chopped and mixed with tiny prawns and scrambled egg, all melded together in a slightly sour yoghurt sauce. Sprinkled on top was a hint of crimson paprika. The mixture was served on a bed of freshly chopped lettuce in frost-coated individual glass bowls. It looked – and tasted – divine.

There, I'm slavering already. But you can see – and almost *taste* – it, can't you? How much better is that description than a mere:

> After an avocado pear starter, they moved on to the main course of . . .

Similar details will help bring alive the clothes your characters wear, the houses in which they live and the rooms in which the scene is unfolding.

Equally, in a historical article, the scene will come alive if I say something like:

> The severed heads, newly-impaled on the rebel pikes, leered obscenely down from the bridge portals. The blood-stained hair of Lord Saye-and-Sele and Sheriff Crowmer hung lankly down below their now-sagging chins. And, on the bridge itself, the battle for London raged on.

That description is surely more 'alive' than a mere statement that the two heads were displayed on the towers of old London Bridge. (It all happened in London during the Jack Cade revolt of AD 1450.)

Personal experiences

I have already mentioned the advantages of recording word-pictures of interesting scenes in an everyday book. Your own experiences, observations and feelings are also well worth recording.

There are several advantages in keeping a – very personal – daily journal. These advantages include:

● You can record your *feelings* about people, your interesting experiences, and your comments on all the things you see. These feelings, experiences and comments will come in useful again and again in your writing life.

● You can note down the ideas for stories and for articles that come to you in flashes of inspiration. Ideas are strictly ephemeral – they come and go with equal speed. (Some sources for ideas are suggested in the Appendix.)

● A daily journal will get you into the habit of writing regularly. You need to exercise your *writing muscle*. If you don't write regularly, you will lose the habit – your writing muscle will waste away.

Personal experiences are meat and drink to article writers. Readers everywhere are interested in reading about other people's experiences – how someone solved a problem, survived an illness or emotional upset, or merely coped with a grandchild. Record all those experiences now, before you forget the details. You will find many uses for them throughout your writing career.

When you come to write them up, the trick is to write about your personal experiences either humorously – which is not as easy as people think – or in such a way that others can learn from your experience. The underlying principle is to tell readers less about what you did and more about what they can do. Which leads us nicely on to your opinions.

Personal opinions

Your experiences are always potentially saleable, inasmuch as others can learn from them, or laugh about them with you. (Or even at you. Never be afraid to let the reader laugh at you, be the butt of your own jokes.)

Your opinions are of less value.

If you are a really well-known personality or an acknowledged expert in your field, then yes, maybe your views are of interest. If you are just an 'ordinary Joe', few will care a jot for what you think. If you want to publicise your far-out political, ethical, moral or religious views … get yourself a soap-box and go make a speech. Don't try to sell your views to magazine editors. They won't buy. Anything that smacks of 'preaching' is a sure-fire candidate for instant rejection.

Accept it, you're in the entertainment business. You're never going to change the world.

Chapter 5:

Market Research

You may look upon your writing as a hobby, but you should still go about it in a business-like manner. If you don't, it won't be a paying hobby – and that's what this book is all about. So let's be business-like.

In this context, what does 'being business-like' entail? It means that you must:

- Submit your work to the *right* market.
- Submit the *right* work to the selected market.
- Submit your work in the *right* way.

Submitting your work will be dealt with in Chapter 11. In this chapter, we will concentrate on finding the right market and offering the right work. And although this chapter immediately precedes that on article-writing, for which it is essential, market research is also important to those who wish to write short stories.

Those who wish to write books – fiction or non-fiction – will need to research their markets too. This is dealt with at the end of this chapter.

First, the magazine market.

Which magazine?

Choosing a magazine to submit your work to is not just a matter of blindly sticking a pin in a list. You must investigate the market and select appropriate magazines to 'attack'.

Initially, you should not target too many magazines at a

time. For a start, select just two or three magazines and concentrate on getting published in these. But the question is still . . . which ones?

Think back to the philosophy outlined in the first chapter. Getting published early in your writing career is important: it will give your writing ego a boost. It is therefore best to attack the magazines which use the most contributed work and attract the least competition from other writers. Adopting that approach, consider the following points:

- Weekly magazines are published 52 times a year, whereas monthlies appear only a dozen times. For a similar-sized magazine, therefore, the weekly one will usually require four times more contributions than the monthly.

- As editorial policy, some magazines use a lot of outside, freelance contributions; others are largely staff-written – or, at least, written by a small team of regular 'known' freelances. When researching the market, the writer should seek to ascertain the source of contributions.

- Local or regional magazines attract less competition from other writers than do national publications. Thus, most contributions to, say, *Sussex Life* will come from writers living in, or near, Sussex. Few Yorkshire writers will be submitting work to *Sussex Life*. But writers living all over the country offer their work to the national magazines.

- Trade, craft and hobby magazines are usually contributed to solely by writers specialising in the trade, craft or hobby. But no writer can be a specialist in everything. As with local magazines therefore, the competition is reduced.

- Many free circulation magazines are in need of material. Take care though: not all such magazines pay for contributions. Find out first.

- The more experienced a writer becomes, the more he or she expects to be paid. The more experienced writers seldom submit work to low-paying markets. This leaves the field clearer for the beginning writer to gain experience.

The best markets for beginners

The logical conclusion from the above is that the beginning writer is well advised to select, as target markets, restricted circulation (by geographical area or by specialism), relatively low-paying, weekly magazines which appear to use largely freelance-contributed material. In an ideal world, that conclusion is correct. In the real world, the choice is not that easy. You may not be able to find, or write for, magazines which fit that specification exactly. But you should aim to get close to it.

Another possible choice of magazine to target initially is the newly launched magazine. Established magazines build up associations with writers; the work of known, experienced writers is inevitably more favourably considered than that of unproven newcomers. Furthermore, established magazines build up reserve stocks of publishable material, waiting for the right opportunity. A newly launched magazine has no such stockpile, and no 'stable' of proven writers. The editor needs material to fill the pages. There can be no gaps.

So watch out for new titles, and get in quick. Maybe you can become one of their regular writers. But beware magazines that 'fold' after a couple of issues!

Finding magazines

It's all very well laying down a philosophy for choosing a target magazine. But how and where can the beginning writer find out about all the magazines that are available?

The first source is obvious: browse through the shelves of your local news-stand/magazine-seller. (This is easiest at railway stations and airport terminals, where plenty of people are killing time . . . browsing.) Be thick-skinned – keep browsing until you are told to move on.

Get to know as many as possible of the magazines that are around. You can flip through the pages of a magazine and quickly get the 'feel' of it. You will know whether you are most likely to be writing for staid, up-market magazines or for brash, popular publications. That choice narrows your selection down considerably. You still have to look at a lot.

Don't forget either, the magazines in office and other waiting rooms. These may be out-of-date but they will be useful enough for a first glance-through. (Don't rely on out-of-date samples though; magazines are always changing.)

Remember too the magazine that you already see regularly. If you are a longstanding reader of (the notional) *Widget Collector*, you may well be able to write for it. You are already acquainted with the typical reader – the person you have to write for. It's someone just like you – with similar likes and expectations.

Market reference books

There are also writers' reference books listing magazines and their basic requirements. In Britain, we have the choice of:

> *Writers' & Artists' Yearbook, annually, A & C Black, and The Writer's Handbook (Ed: Barry Turner) annually, Macmillan.*

The American market is comprehensively covered in two bumper (in size, coverage, and cost) handbooks:

> *Writer's Market, annually, Writer's Digest Books, and The Writer's Handbook, annually, The Writer, Inc.*

Detailed study of a magazine

Let us assume that you have now selected a small number of magazines which you propose to 'attack'. (If you haven't yet selected your targets, let me suggest: a relevant specialist magazine, a county or similar 'nostalgia' type magazine, and a general-interest one.) You will need to have at least two, and preferably three, sequential copies of the selected magazines; a single copy will not suffice. The small number of target magazines is important: if you try to master the needs of too many different magazines you will surely fail.

You must study these few magazines carefully and then keep 'attacking' them, learning from each rejection, until you breach the 'success barrier'. Once you achieve an initial success, you should consolidate. Submit more material to the magazine before the editor has time to forget you. You want to establish yourself as potentially a reliable and regular contributor.

How do you study a magazine, from the viewpoint of a potential contributor? In your initial overview:

- Flip through the pages to get a general 'feel' for the whole magazine. Ask yourself whether it is popular or prestigious, brash or staid, open-minded or prejudiced. Is it a magazine which you would enjoy reading? (If not, perhaps you should choose a different target magazine.) Would you be happy to be published in it?

- Look for the small print at the foot of the 'masthead' page; some magazines carry a note to the effect that they will not even consider – nor return – unsolicited material. The 'masthead' page is usually one of the first few pages, often the Contents page; it is the one which gives the name of the editor – and sometimes of other members of the editorial staff – and the editorial address. It is not impossible to get published in magazines which won't consider unsolicited material, but these are not the best to attack when starting out. Again, perhaps choose a different target magazine.

- Check to make sure that the magazine does in fact publish short stories and/or articles, whichever is your interest. (There are some magazines which publish all stories and no articles; there are many which publish nothing but feature articles. Only the most amateurish of beginner-writers submits a short story to a magazine which never uses them.)

- Study the advertisements. Advertising agencies take great pains to place their clients' advertisements where they are likely to be seen by their 'target purchasers'. Agencies know each magazine's target readership. And if you too are to succeed in writing for that magazine, you too need to know their target readers.

If a women's magazine has advertisements for toddlers' toys, supermarket foodstuffs, and mail order clothes . . . the average reader is probably a young housewife and mother, rather less than affluent. If another magazine has advertisements for French perfumes, designer clothes and expensive cars, the typical reader is . . . rather different, but equally identifiable.

● Check with the Contents page, or use your further samples of the magazine, to identify those features which are 'regulars' – columns on various interests. If a magazine has a regular motoring correspondent, it is unlikely to welcome a general-interest article from you about motoring.

● More difficult than the previous suggestion, try to identify which feature articles are written by the magazine's own staff writers (check on the masthead page), by 'regular' freelances or are specially commissioned. Try to differentiate between staff/commissioned material and that supplied by freelance writers like yourself.

Obvious clues are if the writer's name is recognisable and/or if the article is an interview with a major celebrity. 'Names' seldom write on spec, and unknowns seldom get to interview big stars. It is helpful too to look at the further samples you have of the magazine: if the same writer's work appears again, he or she is probably the recipient of regular editorial commissions or 'go-aheads'.

● Take note of the types of subject dealt with in feature articles and their treatment. One magazine will carry a lot of travel features; another will specialise in advice to improve readers' sex lives. One will use conventional text in its articles; another presents its material in a number of 'bite-sized' snippets. One magazine will specialise in hard factual articles, another in strictly news-related items. Each magazine has its own individual characteristics.

- Similarly, look at the stories the magazine carries. Pay particular attention to the ages of the characters in the stories. (Readers like to identify with the hero/heroine.) Some magazines use only 'short-shorts' (coffee-break stories); some insist on twist endings; some use only romantic stories; some use picture stories (comics style). These different types of short story are looked at in Chapter 7. For now, it is sufficient that you notice the different requirements.

- Take note of how many 'outside' articles and short stories are used per issue. If the number of either is too small then, again, maybe you should choose a different target magazine.

- Check out the Letters page and any Readers' Problems page. Both pages will give good indications of the readership – age, interests, affluence, family background, etc. In the extremes, if many letters refer to the writer's grandchildren, then the readership is likely to be mature/elderly. If the 'Agony Aunt' is fielding questions about teenage romance, then the readership is probably teenaged.

Your own market reference file

You may find it helpful to write up your own market study findings. Many writers develop their own file of target magazines, devoting a page per magazine to notes on target readership, editorial 'slant', overall approach, etc. It is also useful, as you become more experienced, to record the names of your editorial contacts. Fig. 1 (overleaf) shows an example of a 'personal' market study report.

The Lady		**Weekly £1.00**
Editor: Arline Usden		Issues studied
Features Editor: Janina Pogorzelski		4 Oct 20XX
		7 Mar 20XX

39–40 Bedford Street
London WC2E 9ER

www.lady.co.uk	Email: editors@lady.co.uk	Tel: 020 7379 4717

Readership:	Age 40+, female, affluent.
Size:	Average issue has about 80 A4 pages, split roughly 50/50 adverts/editorial.
Adverts:	About ten pages of classified ads for holiday accommodation, home and abroad; half-a-dozen pages of domestic and carer staff opportunities; half-a-dozen pages of OAP-related items – stair-lifts, bath-seats, recliner-chairs, etc.; several 'reader offers'.
Regular columns:	News update ('arty'); Theatre and opera reviews; Gardening; Cooking; Fashion; Personal finance; Well-being; Wine; Puzzles (crossword, sudoku, 'Ladygram', Bridge).
General 'feel':	'Comfortable', affluent, informative, educated/sophisticated tastes. Not brash.

Freelance items

Articles:	About 5 feature articles per issue, about 50/50 one- and two-pagers (900 and 1,200 words) – 3–4 pix with two-pager, sometimes colour, sometimes black and white; usually only one pic, usually black and white, with one-pager. Plus the Viewpoint spot.
Typical topics:	Meeting American Indians (2 pages, 4 colour pix); Cruising Norwegian Fjords (2 pages, 3 colour pix); The Severn Bore (1 page, 1 b/w pic); a vet tells how he was inspired by a parrot (1 page, 1 b/w pic); Searching for Shakespeare's face (2 pages, 4 colour pix – agency). Longer features often include a closing 'factfile'.
Regular opinion spot:	The weekly 'Viewpoint' column (reader-contributed opinion spot, possibly controversial, within reason) – 450 words. Topics include getting over death of a pet and the merits of unusual holidays.
Short story:	One in each issue, averaging about 1,800 to 1,900 words. Not 'romantic' – just good stories. Recently: young lad doing community service, in (60?) woman's garden, for minor offence. She befriends him, despite her daughter's advice. She sells an antique clock; she falls and is knocked unconscious. Lad is accused of stealing clock. Recovering in hospital, she tells daughter that she had sold the clock – not lad's doing at all. Son-in-law gives lad a job. Viewpoint – the older lady.

Fig. 1. A typical 'personal' market study report – on *The Lady*.

One further item of important information is often less immediately available. You need to find out how much the magazine pays for articles and stories.

Many editors are unwilling to specify what they will pay for accepted material. They prefer to negotiate the cheapest rate they can, based on their own assessment of the worth of the article or story. The writer, however, needs to have some idea of the likely payment before perhaps investing a lot of time in research or, in the case of a short story, relinquishing the First Rights.

When dealing with magazines listed in the various reference books (see above) the writer can sometimes get some idea of the likely rates of pay. But more often not. When starting out, as will be explained in Chapter 11, the beginning writer can only offer his or her work for payment 'at your usual rates'. You will, though, quickly build up information on which magazines to continue attacking and which to downgrade in your personal market assessment.

Select a model article

But the overall assessment of the magazines' readership and general slant/approach is not the end of your market research. For your early attempts to breach the success barrier it is helpful to model your work on a piece that has already been submitted.

As you study the potential target magazines, watch out for what you judge to be a freelance-submitted article which appeals to you, and which you think you could emulate. Now study that article in great detail – take it to pieces.

Read it through carefully, several times. Get 'the feel' of it. Notice how the writer has grabbed your attention in the opening paragraph; how he or she has retained your attention throughout; how he or she has left you, at the end of the article, with a feeling of satisfaction, of having reached a good conclusion.

Now study it more mechanistically:

- Count the total number of words in the article. Count them by sentence and paragraph and then tot them up. Where the writer has split sentences with colons or semi-colons, treat these as the end of a sentence; thus, treat this sentence as two, one of 18 words, and the other of 15.

- Count the number of sentences in each paragraph, and notice the variety of lengths – some short, some longer.

- Count the number of paragraphs in the whole article, again noting the variety. The opening paragraph is probably one of the shortest.

- Look for the 'difficult' (i.e. 'long') words that the writer has used. If the article is in a 'popular' magazine, there will be few words of more than three syllables and all unusual words will be explained either specifically or by their context. Discount 'long' words produced by having 'heads' or 'tails' added to them. For example, the four-syllable *dis/es/ta/blish* is merely the easily understandable *establish* plus a prefix.

- Notice how many separate 'stories' or topics are included in the one article. A thousand-word article might consist of six to eight such related items.

   For example, one general-interest article about red-haired people, which I analysed, contained separate story-items – interesting/amusing details – about:
   - the personal and genetic characteristics of those with red hair,
   - the number of hairs on a typical red-head (many fewer than the average),
   - the proportion of red-heads in the general population,
   - famous red-haired people (Napoleon hid his red hair by dyeing it),
   - the number of red-haired American presidents and British sovereigns . . . and so on.

- Notice whether, and how many, anecdotes (usually including dialogue – supposed quotes) are used in the article. Nowadays, many articles in British magazines include illustrative anecdotes.

Having made the above mechanistic check, what do you do with it?

Fashion your early attempts to break into this particular market on the model article you have pulled to pieces. If the model uses twenty paragraphs in a thousand-word article, do the same, more or less – certainly, don't use less than fifteen. If the overall length of the article is 800 words, tailor yours to 800 words too – give or take no more than about 50 words. If no sentences exceed 25 words long, then restrict yours to that length too. Follow the 'pattern' of the model, but without copying it.

The chances are that the style of your model will show a marked similarity to the guidelines outlined in Chapter 3. Naturally. That's how I got there too.

Select a model story

If you wish to write short stories, you need to undertake a similar, but perhaps slightly less mechanistic, exercise. When studying a short story:

● Count the total number of words in the story. Overall length is every bit as important with short stories as it is with articles. No editor wants a story which over-runs the space available. They won't sacrifice revenue-earning advertisements to make room for your story; they'll cut – or, more likely, reject – your story.

Whereas it is preferable to count article-words individually (or rely on the computer's word-count facility), this is not the best way to count story-words. Editors are really interested in the *space occupied* by an article or story. And dialogue uses space differently from straight running text; it tends to produce more short, incomplete lines.

So, take a typical section of a short story – some dialogue, some description – and count the words in, say, twenty lines. This will vary with magazine-column-width: the object is to count at least a hundred words. Calculate the average number of words per line. Count the lines in the whole story and multiply by the words per line. Counting this way allows for the 'dialogue-spaces'.

- Assess the approximate proportion of dialogue to description. This will inevitably vary from story to story and writer to writer but it is useful to get a broad overall 'feel'.

- Note the number of characters involved in the story and whether there are many, or any, peripheral characters. Take careful note of the ages of the characters. Few magazines for teenagers will have granny-characters in their stories (although they creep in occasionally). That's easy to spot: less easy is the differentiation between characters in magazines aimed at teens-and-twenties readers, those aimed at 25-year-olds, and those aimed at 35-year-olds.

- Take note of the social and moral attitudes of story characters. These will vary not just with character-age, but also from magazine to magazine. (The editor of one British women's magazine did not allow short story characters to smoke; another magazine won't allow the story to 'go beyond the bedroom door'; another welcomes relatively explicit love scenes.)

- Take note of the *viewpoint* of the story. Some magazines use mainly first person viewpoint stories; others require the more usual third person viewpoint, some requiring this to be exclusively the heroine's.

- Note how the punch-line is brought in. There has to be a punch-line in a short story.

Once again, for your early attacks on the market, model – but don't copy – your short story along the lines of one in your target magazine. Let your hero and heroine be of similar ages to those in the model; seek to include a similar proportion of dialogue in your story; if your model story has only three characters, you should not use 'a cast of thousands'. And, more importantly, work to a similar length.

There is more about writing short stories in Chapter 7.

Market research – books

Researching into the market for books – both fiction and non-fiction – is a different exercise from the study of the magazine market.

The book-market researcher needs to ascertain:

- Which publishers publish the type of book the writer wishes to write. Some firms publish only fiction, others only non-fiction; some genre fiction only, others 'literary' fiction only; some only textbooks, others just biographies.
- The publishers most likely to look with favour on a book from a new writer. Some publishers refuse to consider unsolicited submissions from new writers. See their websites, the *Writers' & Artists' Yearbook* or *The Writer's Handbook*.
- The preferred, or currently popular, length for the type of book in which you are interested. One publisher of romance stories specifies 50,000 to 55,000 words, another 40,000; against that, hardly any 'mainstream' novels would be considered at fewer than about 70,000 words and family sagas tend to be at least 120,000 words long; the market for 20,000 word novellas is virtually non-existent; an educational book would be a minimum of 35,000 to 40,000 words while other non-fiction books often need at least 60,000 words. But these figures vary over the years. Check for yourself.

Each of the reference books listed on page 50 for information about magazines also provides brief details of book publishers' requirements. But, inevitably, the information is very brief and often vague. One well-known British publisher lists its interests as:

> Fiction, general, cookery, business, crime, health and diet, history, music, paranormal, self-help, biography and autobiography.

That doesn't really help much.

Much more useful are the twice-yearly special issues of *The Bookseller*. Each of these bumper issues, available by subscription only (although you can subscribe merely for the two issues), carries advertisements for most of the leading British publishers, illustrating their next six months' titles. In the text, the forthcoming lists are briefly reviewed across publishers, by category. Each of the special issues is a goldmine of invaluable information on who publishes what. The special issues are very expensive, but your local public library should have a copy that you can browse through. For free.

Once you have a fair idea of the publishers most likely to be interested in the type of book you wish to write, it is worth getting a copy of each of these publishers' catalogues. This can often be achieved by just phoning their offices – the postage costs alone will be hefty – or visiting the annual London International Book Fair (Spring each year) and picking up the catalogues you fancy. Alternatively, study the publishers' websites; most give full details of the books they publish.

Chapter 6:

Writing Magazine Articles

We have already discussed the merits of getting published, getting into print, as early as possible in a writer's career. And maybe you have already achieved this, by writing a 'Letter to the Editor'.

Prior success or not though, now is the time to progress further; with the same intention, to achieve speedy and paid publication.

Why articles?

Having done your market research – as described in the previous chapter – you will have noticed that far more articles are published than stories. A women's or other general-interest magazine may contain two or three short stories; it will also contain several feature articles – half a dozen or more. A specialist-interest magazine will contain only articles. And there are many more specialist-interest magazines than general-interest ones.

Throughout the world, the market for magazine feature articles is many times greater than that for short stories. You will have more chance of having an article accepted and published than of getting into print with a short story.

Article subjects

Now let's concentrate on what you are going to write articles about. Basically, articles can be:

- An account of a personal experience – your own or someone else's.
- Related and interesting facts and figures about ... anything.
- Advice on how to do ... almost anything.

The one thing that all types of article have in common is their factual basis. Articles are true, articles are factual, articles are non-fiction; stories are fiction, stories are 'made up', stories are figments of the writer's skilful, vivid, imagination.

If you are to write factual pieces, you must know the facts. One of the most popular clichés of writing advice is:

Write about what you know.

The fact that this is a cliché does not mean that it isn't good advice; it merely means that it has been repeated frequently. It is repeated so often because it is indeed good advice. But I prefer to extend and qualify it a little. I would advise beginning writers to ...

Know your subject well before writing about it.

But let's stick with the original cliché for a while. What do you know, right now?

What do you know?

'I'm only a housewife, I haven't got anything interesting to write about.' *Rubbish.*

'My job's not interesting, I couldn't write about it.' *Rubbish.*

'I never go anywhere, I couldn't write about interesting places.' *Rubbish.*

Each of these typical excuses is all too common. Beginners always believe they have nothing interesting to write about. They are wrong.

Women's magazines frequently carry articles about everyday housewifely activities; and is there a housewife anywhere who hasn't her own special way of doing something? Other housewives will be interested to read about this. Most occupations have specialist magazines – maybe the beginner can write about some unusual aspect of the job. Anyway, lots of people like to read about other people's jobs. Wherever you live, city apartment or village cottage, mountain top or river mouth, it is unusual – and therefore interesting – to those who live elsewhere.

The above examples aside, many people also have hobbies (exercise, craft or collection) about which they can write. There are magazines about most hobbies, most energetic activities, most crafts, most collectable things. And writing about your hobby has a further plus point: relatively few of your fellow hobbyists will be writers, relatively few writers will indulge in the same hobby as you. By writing about your hobby you have significantly reduced the competition. You have a better chance to get into print than when writing about a general-interest subject. (Not only that: because of the dearth of writers about some hobbies, specialist magazines often pay high rates to those who can provide what they want.)

Straight away then, in terms of subjects, most readers will have something to write about. Something about which they know.

Article ideas

You may know your subject, particularly if it is a personal experience, but you still need an idea on which to base your article. An idea is what turns an ordinary subject into an interesting article. Remember, we writers are in the entertainment business. It is our job, when writing articles, to take an ordinary, perhaps dull, subject and make it interesting.

I saw an amusing personal experience article in a magazine, about learning to ride a bicycle. Learning to ride a bike isn't much of a subject on its own. The writer of the article, a housewife and mother of two teenage kids, made it amusing, interesting and entertaining by explaining how she had felt left out by the rest of the family when they went off on bike rides. She had never learned to ride. She decided she had to learn. She explained how she fell off once or twice, and then got the knack. And – the punch line – she is now a keener cyclist than all the rest of the family.

An idea is also what differentiates between a topic suitable for an article and one suitable for a book. The history of China is a book subject; how to paint a house is a book subject; how to replace a broken pane of glass is, potentially, an article subject; the origins of gun-powder might equally well be an article subject. Article ideas are small – almost bite-sized; book ideas need to be large enough to fill a book.

Ideas are what turn the dullest subject into a good read. Sometimes an idea need be no more than a gripping title, or an interesting opening paragraph.

Suppose I started an article with the words, 'Alexander the Great and I shared a drink,' I'm sure you'd be intrigued. Then I might go on, 'Not directly of course, nor at the same time. But a little tiny part of the water I've just drunk was also drunk by Alexander.'

Then I would go on to explain about the universal and permanent recirculation of water. It's a safe bet that everyone has shared water with any historical figure they care to name. The subject may be dull, but at least the introduction makes it more interesting.

Developing new ideas

Take a subject. Any subject in which you are interested and, for the moment, already knowledgeable. Ask yourself questions about it. Keep asking yourself 'Why?' and 'How?' – just as a child would. (Extend your questioning perhaps to all six of the 'standard' journalists' questions: 'Who?', 'What?', 'Why?', 'Where?', 'When?' and 'How?' They will not all be relevant, but they will all start you thinking.)

Gradually, as you quiz yourself, you should find that you are becoming more and more interested. An idea for an article will come to you. If it interests you, it can be made to interest readers. Just maintain your own enthusiasm.

Next, move on to new subjects.

To article-writers, ideas are as fuel is to motor-cars. Neither works without. So you must spend time thinking of ideas.

Some ideas will come to you in a flash of inspiration. Fine, but make a note of these ideas straight away. Ideas may come in a flash; they are forgotten just as quickly. The best ideas are always 'the ones that got away'.

Work at developing ideas. The question-asking routine mentioned already is one good method. Another way is to look at other people's articles. Say to yourself, 'I could write something like that – on a different subject perhaps, for a different magazine perhaps, but similar.' Look at old magazines too. An article that sold ten years ago can usually be updated, freshly researched, and rewritten for a magazine of today. There's little that's really new, but beware of plagiarism.

Think about cross-fertilising your interests: if you collect stamps and run marathons, how about an article about stamps depicting marathons? Or statues (I 'collect' them) of revolutionaries (I've researched the English ones), or how to organise a writers' club?

But there is inevitably a limit to the number of potential articles you can think up from your personal experience and your own (other) hobby or job. And if you are going to become a successful article-writer, you need to keep on writing. You need more subjects.

Expand your interests

Refer back to the three generalised article-subjects mentioned on page 62. So far we have only considered writing about your own personal experiences and existing hobbies. You can also write about other people's experiences and activities. 'Profiles' are always popular.

And you can write about anything that interests you too. Expand your interests.

Whenever, in your everyday life, you come across a subject that really interests you, develop this interest. Make yourself a mini-expert in the subject. (You don't need to be the world's greatest expert, just to know more about your subject than the average man-in-the-street.) Then, so long as you write *within the limits of your knowledge*, you can write articles about this new interest.

Let me give you an idea of what I mean. I am fascinated by dragons. So I have investigated them: read books about them, photographed them (as statues), generally researched them.

Did you know, for instance, that St. George, the patron saint of England, was a Turk, who never even visited England? Did you know that he is also the patron saint of Moscow? Did you know that most Chinese dragons have no wings, but live in the clouds, whereas European dragons have wings but seldom leave the ground? Did you know that in China, only the Imperial dragon may be shown with five claws? All others have only four – and Japanese dragons only three. A dragon made of terracotta was a popular rooftop decoration – a gable finial – in southern England in the early twentieth century; a few still survive – there's one right in the centre of Brighton.

Undoubtedly, many know more about dragons than I do. But from my limited research, I have written and sold several feature articles about them.

I have done the same – researched and written – about unusual hats, seashells, public holidays, and English 'revolutionaries' (from Queen Boadicea/Boudicca to Mrs Pankhurst), to list but a few.

You can do the same. Pick a subject – *not* my dragons, please – and make yourself a mini-expert.

New subject or old though, you need to have the facts at your fingertips. Don't rely on your memory: memories are fallible. A successful article-writer is someone who collects and 'organises' material, whether it comes from personal experience or from hard research.

Research sources

Before looking at convenient ways to organise, store and access facts though, let us review the sources. Basically, nowadays, you collect facts from the Internet, from books, from other people's articles and from personal observation and experience.

For any new subject, a good place to start looking is, of course, the Internet. There are a number of search engines but currently, in my view, Google is in a class of its own. (For the unaware reader, go to *www.google.co.uk*.) When starting into a new subject though, Google can be somewhat overwhelming – how do you know which of the thousands of references it throws up are the most useful ones for you? Often, you will do better by merely consulting the Wikipedia, a vast, ever-expanding, on-line encyclopaedia: go to *www.wikipedia.org* and click on English.

Alternatively – and as well – there is merit in consulting your own, preferably single-volume, encyclopaedia. A 'hard' copy is often easier to assimilate, and in the one-volume tome the entry will always be briefer. You may need no further information; you may decide that the subject is not worth further research – it may, for you, be too small, or too large, or too academic.

Having confirmed your interest and decided to go ahead, look more widely. Go back to Google and browse. But don't rely solely on the Internet: books too are always worth investigating. Look for a cheap and simple introductory book: an 'Everyone's Guide to . . .' sort of book, usually in paperback. Find out whether there are any children's books on the subject. Don't be too embarrassed to consult children's books: I rely heavily on children's books for 'first reference' use.

I have, for instance, a marvellous two-volume (Ladybird) set of 48-page books, *Kings and Queens of England*, to which I often refer for a quick date. I have another, similar book for ten-year-olds, called *Great Civilisations: China*. This gives an instant listing of the dynasties and their dates – and a lot more.

You will, of course, explore the second-hand bookshops for books about your subjects.

Investigate too, 'remaindered' or 'bargain' books. These are usually low-selling books which publishers sell off to shops at a reduced price in order to retrieve warehouse storage space. Books sometimes sell less well than expected because they are of too narrow an interest, too specialised for the general public. These are often just the sort of books which writers, expanding their own specialist interests and researching future article subjects, want.

Many of the books on my own shelves – particularly those about English revolutions – have come from remaindered stock. (Specialist firm Bibliophile Books issues regular catalogues of brand new but remaindered/bargain books. Go to *www.bibliophilebooks.com* or phone them on 020 7515 9222 to request a catalogue.)

Whether you obtain your information from the Internet or from books, double-check the facts with other references. Mistakes can appear in books and on websites. Make sure you don't include the errors of others in your work.

Not just books

But your research should not be just from the Internet and books. You will also collect interesting and relevant magazine articles by others. You can pick the brains of knowledgeable friends and acquaintances. You will – in time – seek interviews with experts. You will interview other interesting people too, and write about their experiences.

Prepare at least some questions before any interview, but be prepared to explore new avenues, 'off the cuff'. When interviewing experts and knowledgeable friends, always ask whether they know anyone else who might have useful information. Build up chains of specialist contacts. Depending on the subjects you tackle, your contacts will be an important part of your writing work.

You will also wish to visit – research – relevant locations. On such visits, don't forget to take photographs: good, bad or indifferent, they will always be useful.

Many beginning writers overlook the wealth of factual material that is available for free. Watch out for publicity brochures, for informative advertisements, for museum exhibitions and associated leaflets.

I have, for example, in my research files, an advertising

drinks-mat – picked up in a pub – which explains in considerable details, how to tie a bow tie. I'll use this some day, I'm sure.

Remember too that many large firms and organisations employ staff whose job is to meet the specific needs of journalists. Such press, or information, officers will happily give you lots of free information relating to their organisation. Some will be useful. If your interest is ongoing, you can ask to be added to their mailing list.

Press/information officers may also be able to provide you with illustrations. I obtained, free of charge from a lawn-mower manufacturer, a picture of one of the first lawn-mowers ever. This was used to illustrate an article of mine about the history of lawns and lawn-mowing. I was not paid for the illustration, but the article sold more readily because of the accompanying illustrations. But the illustration of articles generally is outside the scope of this book.

Notes

You can often tear an article out of a magazine to keep it – or you can photocopy it. Some reference and specialist books you will buy: either because you *have* to have them, or because they are too cheap to forgo.

But at least some of your research will be from books borrowed from libraries and friends. These books have to be returned. So take notes as you read. Time spent now, on detailed notes, will pay off many times over, in years to come.

As far as possible, make notes on A4 paper. Print-outs from Internet sources and photocopies will usually be on A4 paper too. This way, your files will be tidier than most. If you must make notes on scraps of paper (perhaps when nothing else is immediately available) paste them onto A4 sheets before filing them.

Head each page of hand-written notes with details of the book: not just the title, but also author, publisher, publication date and the ISBN (International Standard Book Number) – which is usually found above the bar code on the back cover.

Note the book page from which you are quoting. Differentiate clearly between your own summaries and paraphrasing of the text, and actual quotations – which you might wish to re-quote later – and ensure that your copying of the quotations is precise.

If you make your notes on a computer, make a hard copy too; your hard disk could fail, or you could change your computer and find the notes are inextricably lost.

Leave plenty of blank space around your notes. Over the years, you will inevitably want to add extra notes or reminders of other references. Blank space not only accommodates such further notes, but also makes the notes easier to absorb.

Depending on the volume of notes and other research material you accumulate, you need to file it all carefully and retrievably. Many writers, at least initially, store their research material in recycled A4-size envelopes with the contents marked on the outside. My own material is stored in transparent plastic folders of the same size. Other people, with large amounts of research material, store all A4 sheets in date-consecutive lever-arch or box files, recording the contents of each sheet on a card index or similar.

It matters not how you do it, so long as you can readily find that note you made, say, five years ago. Your notes are your bread and butter. They will be the source of future articles.

The article's structure

So, you have an idea for an interesting and entertaining article. You have collected all the necessary facts. You have studied the chapters on style and descriptiveness. And, from your market research, you have a pretty good idea of which magazine is likely to be interested in your article.

What you must do now is consider the structure of your article: the sequence in which you present the information. What are you going to start with, to catch the readers' interest – the hook? How are you going to round it all off at the end? Whatever happens you cannot add in a new thought out of sequence: the whole article must present the information in a logical fashion. (You can't say, as one might in conversation, 'Oh, by the way, I forgot to tell you earlier . . .')

Among the commonly-used structures for feature articles are:

- The chronological or calendar structure – first you do this, next you do that; or this happened, then this, and then that. This structure is usually essential for instructional features. It is also often used in describing historical events – but these can sometimes incorporate a 'flashback' technique. This would enable you to start your article with a really 'grabby' hook, and explain its relevance/origins subsequently. An example of this might be something like: 'The battle raged to and fro across the bridge; gradually the 'Blues' overwhelmed the 'Reds'. It had all started several months before, when . . .'

- The circular structure – start with an interesting fact, expand on it and then close with a reference to how the initial fact can be affected. This gives the reader a satisfactory conclusion – all is nicely rounded off. An example of this might perhaps be an opening statement about the number of road traffic accidents expected in the coming year – and then the article rounding off with the statement that, if all the measures outlined in the article are adopted, there would only be half as many.

- The 'Twin Peaks' structure – start with some surprising information and have another near-equally (or even more) surprising fact to close the article with. This approach is particularly relevant when the article is to be a collection of interesting facts on a single topic. I have written such articles about dragons, about hats, about sea-shells – each recounting a number of related facts, on the one subject.

Think hard about the structure of your article: a good structure leads the reader along a logical path to full understanding; a poor structure can deter or 'lose' the reader, and thus ruin an otherwise good article.

Article outlines

Increasingly, magazine editors are requiring to see an outline of an article before they will consider the full piece. (I would not recommend a full outline as described below for articles of fewer than 700 words: either submit the finished piece or merely mention, in a single paragraph within an enquiry letter, the main points to be covered in it.)

An article outline should not exceed a single page of type-script, single-spaced. It should consist of:

- The proposed title.
- The 'hook' – just one or two paragraphs, maybe 70 words in all.
- A list of sub-topics to be covered in the article, in the proposed sequence (based on the pre-decided structure).
- Possibly, if already determined – or a particularly good punch-line – the brief closing paragraph; no more than say 50 words, and the shorter the better.
- The proposed length of the piece. (This shows the editor you know the length he is likely to prefer and gives him the opportunity to vary the requirement.)
- The availability of suitable illustrations (maybe enclose/ attach a copy – never the original – of one of the illustrations).
- The writer's credentials and/or 'qualifications' (experiential rather than academic) for writing the article.
- The writer's contact details – postal address, phone number, email address.

Ready, steady, go

Submit your outline to the editor of your chosen target magazine. And wait. Unfortunately, not all magazine editors bother to respond to article outlines. If they like it, they will, fairly quickly; if they don't, an outline may go straight into the waste-bin. Give an editor three or four weeks to consider an outline and if there is still no reply, assume the worst.

But let's be optimistic. The editor liked your outline. Unless you are already known to the magazine, you are unlikely to get more than, 'That sounds interesting. I'd like to see the finished article.' No commitment, but if your article lives up to the promise in the outline, it stands a good chance of acceptance.

The article is fully researched and planned. You've got an interested editor. All you have to do now is write it. And don't leave it too long – get the finished piece to the editor within about a couple of weeks. Leave it any longer and he may well have forgotten all about his earlier interest.

As you write, keep thinking about your readers. Are you keeping them interested/amused? Or the ultimate kiss of death – will they just yawn and ask, 'So what?'

Copyright

Beginning writers always worry about copyright. This is understandable and right. But don't worry too much. As long as you write up your own ideas in your own words, you won't go far wrong:

- There is no copyright in ideas. It is not uncommon for several writers to come up with similar ideas at the same time, all perhaps sparked by the same programme on TV.
- There is no copyright in facts. If you take all your facts from a single source though, you may be in danger of accusations of plagiarism – using the fruits of someone else's work. Carry out your research, no matter how small the subject, from several independent sources to safeguard against this. And make sure that the words in which you express the facts are your own. Don't copy.
- When you submit an article, you are (usually) assumed to be offering the right to use it first, and once only. You sell First British (or American, or World, or whatever) Serial Rights. (For more on this see Chapter 11.)

Chapter 7:

Writing Short Stories

I have already made the point that you'll have more chance of success if you write articles. But you really want to write stories.

And ... well ... short stories are shorter than novels, so you think you'll start with short stories. 'Short stories will be "easier" than full-blown novels, won't they?' No. They may take less time to complete because they're shorter. But easier? No.

Let me clarify. Novels and short stories are both fiction, both the product of a writer's imagination. Apart from that, they are very different. A short story is not a novel told briefly; a novel is not an expanded short story.

A short story tells of a few moments in time, a period when a character changes in some way – when something *happens*. A short story usually explores just one facet of a character's personality. A short story does not relate a whole life, merely one episode – but an important one. A short story is short and pointed. A novel has to fill a broad canvas: it needs plots and sub-plots, it depicts many scenes. It shows the whole person (persons) – the good, the bad, and the ordinary characteristics. A novel is ... full and rounded.

How long?

The length of a short story is, of course, a variable feast. Your market research will have given you some insight into the story length required by the markets you hope to attack. A good *average* length today might be around 2,000 words – but there is a seemingly ever-growing demand for the 800- to 1200-word 'short-short' or 'coffee-break' story. For these stories you must write closely to the individual magazine's required length. (Gone – at least in the popular press – are the days of the 10,000-word short story. There are few openings for short stories in excess of 4,000 words.)

One reason why a short story is difficult is that the writer has to establish setting, atmosphere, tension, character, and tell the story – and all in the space of just one or two thousand words. To do this successfully requires high-quality writing. The construction of a short story has to be tight – precise. The words have to be just right. There is no room for a slow build-up. In some ways, a novel may be easier.

Markets for short stories

As always, as serious practitioners in the entertainment business, we should decide in advance the market we are writing for. Short stories can be written for:

- Women's magazines.
- General-interest and 'literary' magazines.
- Teenage, and younger children's magazines and 'dedicated' pages in women's magazines.
- Science fiction magazines.
- Reading on radio.
- Competitions.

In the English-speaking world, the greatest number of openings for short stories are currently found in women's magazines. If you hope to achieve success in the short story field today, you must write for the market of today.

That may not be as onerous as it will at first appear to many men. Men do write for women's magazines – and under their own names too. And, although many women's magazines feature a preponderance of romantic stories, this is by no means essential. Many now welcome 'straight' crime, mystery or ghost stories – or the same with a romantic element.

And twist-ending stories are universally welcomed. Virtually all magazines for women readers though, still require mostly female lead characters (for reader identification, see below).

Apart from women's magazines

There are, of course, still some 'literary' magazines that use short stories. But such magazines are few and far between, are usually inundated with submissions, and hence tend to pay very low rates.

Opportunities exist for short stories for children and teenagers. Writing for teenagers is a skill of its own: it is hard for a middle-aged writer to write so that a teenager of today can identify with the story. Not impossible, but hard. There are a few opportunities for short stories aimed at Mum or Grandma reading to a toddler – such opportunities are, of course, within women's magazines. And there are a few opportunities for writing picture story scripts – comic strips – for children. (See below.)

The one field where male-oriented (and that comment will get me into trouble with all the excellent lady SF writers) other-than-romantic short stories are still, and always, welcomed is science fiction. Science fiction short stories are alive and very well. Not only are there the relatively glossy, well-established science fiction magazines and the 'pulps' (newsprint magazines), but also many *fanzines* – low-paying but excellent 'apprenticeship' markets. If you are 'into' SF, try writing it.

There are also a few magazines taking crime short stories – in Britain though, these are mostly low-paying markets. (Investigate *Crimewave*. See *www.ttapress.com*.)

Radio too is often a major market for short stories. In Britain there are frequent fifteen-minute short story spots on national radio: fifteen minutes means about 2,300 words. Local radio too often welcomes short stories – but they may not pay for them.

The market for short stories may be declining overall, but it is still very much there. At least for now.

What makes a short story?

Having already explained that a short story is about a moment of change, let's be more specific. A short story is made up of:

- Characters – with whom the reader can identify.
- Conflict – the essential ingredient.
- Resolution of the conflict – by, or leading to, the change in the character.

Before any of these three essential ingredients will 'fit together' though, the writer needs a basic idea, the *theme* perhaps, which the story illustrates.

The theme for a short story is usually a simple one. Proverbs, morals and clichés are often sources for themes: 'pride comes before a fall', 'crime doesn't pay', or 'there ain't no such thing as a free lunch' (succinctly remembered, with thanks to SF Master-writer Robert Heinlein, as TANSTAAFL), etc.

Sources of ideas

The idea might not start with a theme. But an idea you must have. If you haven't an idea around which to spin your story, you've just got to get one. Consider the following possibilities (and check the Appendix for more):

- Take an interesting news item and extend it: play 'What if . . .?' Similarly, study magazines' 'agony columns' – the readers' problems pages. These are a never-ending source of short story ideas.
- Think of a nursery rhyme and translate the action into the present day. (Who's sleeping in Goldilocks's bed now?)
- Read just the introductory blurb about a published short story – and write your own story from that blurb. As long as you don't read the original story, yours will always be different.

● Try lateral thinking – things may not be quite what they seem.

Whatever the source, you must decide what your story is to be about: what universal truth you are to illustrate – basically, what's going to happen.

Now we come back to the basic content of the short story. The first element is the characters.

Characters

Your short story is going to be about people. (If not, it's going to be about anthropomorphic animals, or aliens, or whatever, but behaving like people.) And your characters must be believable.

Some story-writers collect news and advertisement pictures of interesting-looking people who can become their characters. Pick a picture, and think of your hero or heroine as looking like that while you write your story. Plenty of novelists – more often than short story writers who work to a shorter time-scale – actually keep pictures of their main characters pinned up in front of them while they write.

Before you start to write you must know your characters as well as you know your best friend. (Better even, for you will know all your characters' secrets.) It may also help to scribble out a very brief character description before you start writing. But don't spend too long on such preparatory work – for a short story it should all be in your head. Indeed, once you know your characters well, a story will often come to mind merely by thinking how they would react to an imposed situation.

As you can see, the theme, the idea, the characters, the conflict, and the resolution are all interwoven. It is hard to tell which is the chicken and which the egg.

The characters in your story have to be believable. Think about yourself, think about your partner, think about anyone you know well. At first thought, we may think ourselves just 'ordinary'; but think a little more. No one is all good, nor all bad. Every person is an *individual*. Every believable character has - like Oliver Cromwell - one or two warts, but not necessarily physical ones.

If you say, 'Colonel Fitzwilliam was a short, stocky little man who habitually wore a tweed jacket and cavalry twill trousers', the good Colonel is a mere 'cardboard' character. But mention that 'he had a nervous habit of pulling at his wine-red nose' and he becomes more of an individual. We have added flesh to the cardboard. Similarly, David could be a rugged macho hero: he comes more to life though, when you mention that he's scared stiff of spiders - or wears glasses. Give your characters 'warts' and they will come alive. Maybe make the 'warts' you mention relevant to the story you are telling.

A short story should have no more characters than are strictly necessary. The fewer you can manage with, the better the story.

Conflict

Without a conflict you don't have a short story. More likely you just have an anecdote, a recounting of a personal experience. This is a typical beginner's mistake. A short story must have - as above - believable characters, a conflict involving them, and a resolution. Without conflict, there is no drama. And drama is what people read short stories for.

Conflict in a short story does not have to be a display of fisticuffs or a taking up of arms. (There's enough of that outside the bounds of the short story.)

Conflict can be a difference of opinion over money; it can be a character's resistance to an emotional attraction; or mankind against the elements; or coping with an unfaithful spouse. Conflict can be a character's battle with his/her conscience - being torn two ways. Or it can be simply the difficulty of making an important decision.

Whatever the conflict, it has to be something that can be resolved - by the characters themselves. You must not, in any form of fiction, and particularly in a short story, resolve the problems, the conflict, by a coincidence or accident. No editor will accept the resolution that 'it was all a dream'. The resolution must be something that springs, apparently naturally, from the personality and character of the protagonist(s). And by resolving the problem on their own, the characters learn something about themselves.

Plot and structure

When you have thought through the basics of your story – the characters, their relationships, the conflict and its resolution, you just about have the plot. And because a short story is just that – short – you need a carefully determined plot; if for no other reason, to ensure that there are no loose ends.

The plot – the story-line – ties together the various essential ingredients. The plot tells you, ready for the start of the actual writing, where the story is going.

The structure tells you how it gets there – keeps you on track. The structure of a short story is elementary (but too often overlooked) and threefold. A short story should consist of:

1. A beginning.
2. A middle.
3. An end.

In the beginning, you must:

●   Provide the hook – something to seize the reader's instant attention. (Ideally, within the first couple of sentences.)
●   Set the scene – establish where, and in some cases when, the story takes place.
●   Introduce the leading characters.
●   Establish the background to the problem (maybe the problem itself).

Often, either in the beginning section or early on in the middle, you will also need to:

- Plant a clue to the final resolution – mention the personality characteristic which blossoms perhaps, or hide an important fact within a longer description.

In all cases, the story should start as near to the end as possible. Include only the minimum of pre-problem activity – of 'back-story'. Jump straight in: it's a short story. The shorter the overall time-span the better, and the easier to manage. Too many (unacceptable) short stories don't start until page 2 of the typescript.

If you just *must* provide some back-story, this can sometimes be achieved by a *flashback*. The viewpoint character 're-lives' the past:

> It had already been one of those disaster days at work when Elaine first tripped over Joe's foot. He had sidled in, smiling shyly ... [add the rest of the back-story – then ...] That had been just last Friday. Today, everything was marshmallow pink. Elaine was floating ...

Notice the use of the word *had* at the start and finish of the flashback. You don't need to remain in that tense throughout the flashback, as long as you make clear when it starts and ends.

In the middle section of your story, you must:

- Introduce the problem and the conflict.
- Outline the first unsuccessful attempts being made to resolve the problem.
- Describe the characters' feelings as the lead character fails – again – to resolve the problem. (Milk the situation for all the emotion you can extract.)
- Pile on more and more suspense – how *can* the problem be resolved?
- Suggest a solution – which may hinge on a difficult, personality-changing, decision by the lead character.

In the end section, which may be very brief, you have to:

- Show how the conflict/problem is resolved – by the actions of the protagonists.

The end section need/should not be long-drawn-out: once the lovers are finally together, the reader doesn't need to be told that they then lived happily ever after. Avoid creating an anti-climax. What is important is that the reader feels satisfied. (The worst thing is for the reader to finish reading and say, 'So what?')

Viewpoint

Earlier, I mentioned the reader's wish to identify with the lead character in your short story. The reader wants to *live* the romance, or whatever – vicariously.

You can assist the reader in this, which will lead to greater satisfaction with your writing, by your choice of viewpoint. The viewpoint is that of the character telling the story. The storyteller can only recount what the viewpoint character can see, think or experience. Choice of viewpoint can be most important – the story becomes that person's 'tale'. Sometimes the same basic story can be told more than once – by changing the viewpoint.

In earlier times, authors often wrote from the omniscient viewpoint. In a truly godlike manner, they let the reader in on everything that was going on – on everyone's thoughts and feelings – even adding 'authorial comments'. (In a novel, where the viewpoint often changes, an occasional omniscient section is sometimes acceptable, but not in a short story. There is more on viewpoint in the next chapter – Writing a Novel.)

More customary nowadays in short stories is the single person viewpoint. This single viewpoint can be that of the first, or third person: 'I' or 'he/she'. The single third person viewpoint is that most commonly used in short stories; the third person is usually, but not always, the leading character. The third person viewpoint avoids the over-use of the personal pronoun, which can easily look wrong.

Names

Just as the viewpoint you choose for your story is important, so too are the names you give to your characters. Polly or Abigail would not behave like Tracey or Sharon. We assume that Polly and Abigail are from the nineteenth century; Tracey and Sharon are from the 1980s. They will have differing attitudes. Or maybe Polly and Abigail were the offspring of tradition-loving parents? Even the reason for a character's name starts the storytelling juices flowing.

Apart from the date and the age of the character, the name can also suggest a personality. Colonel Eldon Umberton-Smythe would probably be a rather pompous person; he doesn't sound right as a macho mercenary. The mercenary might be better named something like John Savage. Priscilla Blenkinsop sounds definitely cooler and more 'up-market' than Tracey Smith, who is a bit of a 'raver'. Similarly, Julian sounds more 'precious' than Tom, Dick or Harry.

Make sure, right from when you start describing your characters to yourself, that you give them appropriate and timely names. Then they will come alive in character.

Writing the story

By now, you know your characters: you know the troubles you are going to put them to; you know more or less how they are going to resolve their difficulties; you are about ready to write. Just before you dash off a few thousand carefully chosen words though, stop for one more moment.

There is a (large) school of thought – including Edgar Allan Poe among its more senior members – which recommends that you always know how your story is to end before you start writing. Your story must not just fizzle out like a damp squib, it must go out with a bang. Some writers actually write out the ending before they start, pin it up in front of their desk, and work towards it.

Your ending must:

- Satisfy, without cheating. A not-previously-revealed fact, or 'and then she woke up', is cheating.
- Fit the mood and subject-matter.
- Provide a surprise of some kind, but nevertheless . . .
- Be logical – i.e. be inevitable but unpredictable.

Another useful pre-writing tip is to think of a title. The title of a short story is always most important. It could be the final touch which sells it – or doesn't. You may have to wait until you have finished the story before you can come up with the title – but try. Knowing the title in advance can help you to write the story. You could say . . . **The title is vital.**

How much dialogue?

Many beginners worry about the dialogue in their stories. And it is important. But don't worry. It is of equal importance in novel-writing, so there is a lot about it, to come, in Chapter 9.

Beginners worry particularly about the *amount* of dialogue. Should there be about one-third dialogue, or more, or less? The answer is that it doesn't really matter: use the amount of dialogue that is right for your story. A lot of dialogue may keep the story moving; less may mean an introspective tale.

You've now skipped ahead to the dialogue chapter, studied that, and come back to this one, bursting to go, to write your story. OK. Off you go. You're on your own.

Once you've got your story down 'on paper', the real work starts. Refer back to Chapter 3 (page 38); now you must polish your story, make it an 'easy read'.

Polishing

Read your story aloud – particularly the dialogue – and make sure it all reads easily, that none of the phrases sticks on your tongue, unwilling to be spoken aloud. Don't write down to your reader – but avoid unusual words if possible.

If any passage seems nicely poetic and flowery to you . . . delete it and rewrite.

Ask yourself whether it all *flows* or whether it is disjointed, abrupt and jumpy. Ask yourself whether the characters are real. If they're not real to you, their creator, how can you expect them to come alive for the reader?

Check that all the essential clues have been planted – not too obviously, but in the right spots. Check too that you have not included irrelevant information; there is no room in a short story for anything that doesn't actually move the story forward.

Check that the beginning is gripping enough. If you don't grab the reader's attention in the first hundred words, you'll never get it.

Finally, check the total length. Most of us write too long – and it's usually not difficult to cut to the required length. Remember, many a short story is rejected simply because it's too long.

Competitions

Finally, in relation to conventional short stories, a word about competitions. Competitions can be an excellent way for an up-and-coming writer to break into the short story market. Competitions should not be disdained or overlooked.

When you submit your short story to an over-worked magazine editor it will – eventually – be read, but seldom with much initial enthusiasm. The pile of unsolicited story manuscripts from unknown writers is ever large, forever growing and seldom productive. A competition though is a one-off activity: entries are often judged by a paid outside 'expert'; and, surprisingly, there are often fewer entries than expected. And, most important of all, few top short story writers enter competitions. There is therefore more chance for the new writer to get a foothold.

If you win a prize in an open short story competition, your work sometimes gets published – and may be noticed. Your future chances with editors are possibly enhanced.

The three basic rules for competition entries are:

1. Read and comply with the rules.
2. Read and comply with the rules.
3. Read and comply with the rules.

More competition entries are thrown out for non-compliance than for any other reason. Their quality is immaterial if they aren't eligible. Comply with the entry rules and you're half-way there. And the discipline of working to the competition requirements – subject parameters, opening words perhaps, length, deadline, etc. – is excellent training for any short story writer.

Picture stories

Now let's leave the conventional short story and look at a different, but related, writing field. The picture story. And, no, the writer does not have to draw the pictures.

In essence, the usual one- to four-page picture story is a short story. Instead of leaving it to the readers' imaginations to 'flesh out' the author's descriptions, the setting, the action and the appearance of the characters are all in the pictures. Only thoughts and dialogue – plus an occasional few words to explain the setting or the passage of time – are given as text.

The writer still has to describe the scenes though. The artist (or sometimes a photographer, but photo-stories, once popular, are seldom seen now) has to be instructed, and the story must still be a story, about believable characters.

But first, as usual, the market research. We're talking mainly about comics. And comics are slowly disappearing – the survivors are mainly what might be called the 'real' comics, like *The Dandy* and *The Beano*. The stories are ... fun – they're comics. And there are a few more titles, aimed at younger children.

At the time of writing though, there were a few other publications using picture stories: importantly *2000 AD*, the futuristic comic which has famously outlasted its own 'sell-by date' and survived. And there are the 64-page action picture story books published – up to eight a month – in the COM-MANDO series.

Apart from the COMMANDO stories, which are nearly all 'one-offs', many of the picture stories in the other magazines are about characters who appear in every issue. Do not, though, automatically assume – as, quite reasonably, one might – that a character's regular appearance means that all the stories featuring that character are written by a single commissioned or staff contributor. Magazines themselves often own all the rights in the characters featured in their pages; individual episodes are sometimes written by a number of writers – and can be offered speculatively. Enquire of the magazine's editor whether or not speculative episodes would be welcomed. You could get a pleasant surprise. Some magazines are desperately in need of (acceptable) picture story scripts.

Furthermore, if you have an idea for a series of stories about a new character, suitable for the magazine's readership, you can offer to write the series. (Until you have a 'track record' in the field though, you would probably need to prove your ability by offering a number of scripts *on spec* before the first one is accepted. This is not unreasonable: the editor cannot afford to start a series that then quickly dies on him, due to the writer's inexperience or lack of ability.)

Picture story scripts

To write the script for a picture story you need to think visually – to think in scenes. Initially, with short picture stories, it often helps to draw up one or more sheets of paper with the necessary number of picture-boxes on each. Each of the 'boxes' is usually referred to as a 'frame'. (A single-page picture story will often consist of six frames; seldom are there more than nine frames on a page. Even the longer non-serial stories are usually complete in three or four pages – less than 30 frames.)

Back-story: 10-year-olds Nick and Andy are mates, they live next door to each other. They're in trouble. Earlier in the story, they helped a mature lady with her shopping, missed the school bus – and arrived late at school. (At the end of the story, the lady turns out to be in charge of the museum.) Nick, Andy and the teacher (a man) would have been briefly described at the start of the script.

The script

Frame 5:	Foreground, Nick and Andy in classroom, sitting together. Teacher is talking to class – other boys visible. Nick looks angry.
Caption:	Later ...
Teacher:	Tomorrow we'll visit the museum – if Nick and Andrew can manage to arrive on time!
Nick (THKS):	Sarcastic old so-and-so! We were helping ...
Andy (quietly):	Leave it, Nick.

Fig. 2. The script and resultant picture for a single frame within a children's comic.

Having drawn up the blank, squared-up pages, try to visualise each of the pictures in turn, bearing in mind that each picture must move the story forward. Not only that: the story must fill – but not go beyond – the available number of frames. There is no room in a picture story for the quiet contemplation of one's navel. Something always has to be happening.

With shorter stories, I often actually sketch in – on my sheet of empty boxes – what I want each frame to show. I'm no artist: I draw ovals for close-up faces and stick-men for more distant action. No one other than me ever sees these rough sketches; they are merely to help me describe the scenes.

Once you are clear in your mind how the story is to fit into the available frames, for each frame you must provide:

- A description of the scene – always the setting and the action, and, initially, the characters too – from which the artist will work. (Don't go into too much detail though. Leave the artist scope to use his own imagination. He knows his job – and how to do it most effectively.)

- All the words that the characters are saying – and thinking – in the scene. Speech is shown in balloons, thoughts are shown in bubbles. Avoid having more than one 'speech' per character, and keep all speeches short. Aim at no more than about 25 words *in all* within each frame – dialogue and/or thoughts from the characters, plus . . .

- Any additional caption – e.g. 'next day' or 'meanwhile, back at home' – that may be necessary. Use as few captions as possible.

Back-story:	Mike, a young British boy in China, sees his parents killed by a Japanese officer. He vows revenge, runs away and acquires great fighting skills from a master. Together, they form a guerrilla band to harass the invading Japanese. Later, a British Army intelligence officer, Captain Bob Keaping, is sent, with an assistant, Yau Chai, into China to establish contact with, and offer help to, the anti-Jap resistance. They hear of Mike's group and are looking for them
	....
Pic 46:	Yau Chai and Keaping have 'rescued' their mule and are leaving the café. They are outside – away from the old man – where they have been surreptitiously button-holed by the eavesdropping café owner.
Panel:	The old man knew little, but the café-owner had more information for them.
Café-owner:	Jap soldiers definitely in north, sirs. Maybe five days' walk. Around here, many bad bandit gangs, sirs. You take care. If trouble, say you friend of me – Chin Hwa. I know many good bandits. They help.
Keaping (THKS):	Fishy customer, this one. I don't trust him.
Pic 47:	Keaping and Yau Chai are again walking, followed by their laden mule. Now though, the countryside is very different. They are walking on narrow bunds through flooded fields of rice. Not far ahead of them, a small clump of trees almost like an island among the padi fields. We can *just* spot men hiding in among the trees. As they walk on, Keaping is easing back, towards the mule's pack.
Panel:	Bob Keaping's judgement of the helpful café-owner had been correct. The two British Intelligence agents were walking into an ambush . . .
Yau Chai:	I think there are bandits awaiting us, just ahead, Bob. In the trees.
Keaping:	You're right. I see them. Keep moving – then play for time. I've got a surprise for them.

Fig. 3. The original script for two frames/pictures within the *Commando* picture-story *Murder Hunt* and, opposite, the two resultant pictures. Notice the editorial changes to the text.

Murder Hunt - extract

The many 64-page COMMANDO war stories which I have written required a slight variation in the above advice. Longer captions were extensively used, to move these much longer action stories along. Captions were often 25 words long on their own – but I still endeavoured to hold down the dialogue and thoughts to no more than 25 words per frame.

Fig. 2 illustrates the scripting for a 'normal' short picture-story – and the resulting frame. Fig. 3 shows the script I prepared for just one page in a COMMANDO story, and its published version. Note the editorial changes too.

Chapter 8:

Writing a Novel

The world is full of people who believe that, 'My interesting life would make a marvellous novel – far better than all that glitzy sex and jet-set shopping you get in novels nowadays.' Some actually start writing this potential bestseller. Few finish. Even fewer get published. Novels are difficult to write.

And real life is not what novels are about. Real life is (often) a mess: a novel is a controlled, carefully organised and well-rounded story.

The writing of a publishable novel is hard work. You have to give it a lot of thought and do much careful planning before you start. A novel should be larger than life – but not too obviously so. Few lives are different enough to maintain reader-interest throughout the 70,000-plus words that make a novel. If you don't at least think your novel through before you start it, you may well discover – a quarter of the way into it – that the 'story' is never going to sustain a complete book. You'll have wasted your time. A lot of time. A lot of hard work.

Before we get onto the planning of a novel though, let's look first at prospects and do some market research.

Novel opportunities

Brutally, it is difficult to get a first novel published. It needs not just talent, but a lot of luck too. (Some of that 'luck' can be manufactured by a careful study of the market. Too many first novelists offer their stories to the wrong publishers. But you still need some real luck too – you need someone to recognise your talent.) There is an illustration often given about the chances of becoming a successful novelist. The figures are of course inaccurate – and probably optimistic – but the principles are correct.

1,000,000	people (possibly even 10 million) believe 'they could write a terrific novel if they tried'.
100,000	people actually start to write their novel – they then drop off, chapter by chapter, like flies, as they discover how much hard work is entailed.
1,000	writers – at most – get to complete their novel.
100	authors manage to sell their novel – many who finish never even submit their story to a publisher.
10	first novels 'do quite well' – that is, sell enough copies to cover the advance. (See Chapter 11.)
1	first novel becomes a bestseller – and that takes an awful lot of luck.

'Straight' or genre

Many first-time novelists (want to) write what is effectively a 'straight' or 'literary' novel. But 'straight' novels are far more difficult to sell than are so-called genre novels. The phrase 'genre novels' refers to those novels that fit snugly into the booksellers' (often overlapping) categories: crime, romance, science fiction, fantasy, horror, thrillers, historical/family sagas, and Westerns (cowboys). (Children's novels are not thought of as fitting into the main genres: they are more a genre of their own.)

Your first novel – be it 'straight' or genre though – will almost certainly not make you rich. You can expect an advance of between £1,000 and £5,000. In many cases the royalties from sales will not cover the advance. (Chapter 11 looks into such things as advances and royalties.)

So, for your 70,000 words, which probably took a full year of your spare time to write, you could be paid around £50 per thousand words. (Once again, the title of this book – *The HOBBY That Pays* – is justified.)

The novel to write

The more you can reduce the odds against you with your first novel then, the better. And the first step on that path is probably to aim at writing a genre novel. But it is no good striving to write a type of novel with which you are not happy. The 'failed-writers club' is full of people hypnotized by the thought of the riches earned by some romance writers – but who 'wouldn't dream of reading that rubbish myself'.

It is important also to write your novel within just one genre. Novels which fall between two or more genre 'stools' tend to fail.

Think now about your own reading habits. Most likely you read more of one type of book than another. Most likely it will fit into one of the genre categories outlined above. If that is the type of book you prefer to read, surely it will be the type of book you could best write? You know what goes into such books. You know what 'makes them tick', what makes them popular, at least with you.

If on careful consideration, your favourite books are still 'straight' literary novels, then you've got problems. Have another look at the genres. Maybe you've never considered reading them: try a dozen or so – you may find you enjoy them. But if you're then still stuck on the 'straight' novel, so be it – although a genre novel would have been easier to sell.

Let's look at the novel as a concept . . .

The makings of a novel

In the previous chapter the differences between short stories and novels were explained. But there are, too, many similarities. And the items/concepts which go to make up any story are inevitably similar.

A novel needs:

- An idea or theme (in America, some think in terms of a *premise* – which seems much the same as a theme).

- Strong, identifiable characters.
- An interesting, believable setting – both geographical and, within that, a specific locale.
- Conflict, more conflict, and then still more conflict – which, eventually, is all logically resolved.

The similarities with the ingredients of a short story are obvious: a novel just needs a lot more of everything. (Well, it does have to fill a lot more pages.) And, as with a short story, the ingredients run together.

The originating spark

The theme – which I always find a difficult concept – in genre novels, tends to be more or less standard. In a romance, the theme is usually something like, 'true love conquers all'; in a crime novel, 'crime doesn't pay'. In such instances, the theme is less relevant than in a 'straight' novel. (Which may be why I find the concept of a theme confusing: my fictional interests and reading are almost exclusively in the genres.) Of more importance is the originating spark, the idea . . . whatever it is that makes you want to write the story.

Before you can start on your novel – any novel – you need the originating spark or idea.

Frederick E. Smith (author of the best-selling *633 Squadron*) has explained how one of his later novels, *Of Masks and Minds*, was sparked off by a newspaper story about a new brain surgery technique for curing clinical depression.

Jean Saunders, author of a hundred historical and romantic novels (using a variety of pen-names), describes how she got the idea for her teenage novel *Roses All The Way* from an overheard remark – a harassed mother sending her child to the shops for a loaf of bread, '. . . and don't come home if you lose the money.'

Plots and sub-plots

The initial idea is not enough, on its own though, for a novel. It needs development – the spark must be developed into a plot or storyline. The basic idea is not a plot. The plot comes from the characters: how they act and react – to each other, to the problems and conflicts, and within the setting. Stories are about people – in interesting situations.

Whereas a short story is usually about the change in personality of a single character, a novel is about a number of inter-relating characters. Many of the characters in a novel – all of the leading ones – and their relationships will develop during the course of the story. A character who does not change or develop is a cardboard character – or isn't central to the story.

All the skills and techniques used in bringing to life the characters in a short story are equally relevant in a novel. And you will need more characters. Initially, make notes about your characters. Later, you should expand these into a mini-biography of each of the leading characters. Get to know them as well as you know yourself. Indeed, you will yourself *become* each of the characters in turn as they/you live their lives in the pages of your novel.

The skill of the novelist lies in the weaving together of the changing lives of the separate personalities – in plot and sub-plot. A full-length novel needs more than a single plot: it needs a good strong main story, but this in turn needs the support of one or more lesser – subsidiary, but associated – stories.

In a novel, the setting too is most important. A particularly romantic – or horrific – setting alone can sometimes spark off an idea for a story.

Conflicts and crises

Most of all though, once the characters are alive in your mind, the essential ingredient of a novel is conflict. Remember, the conflicts need not be physical; conflict can also be:

- Against the environment (storms, etc.) or the location (stranded perhaps).
- With the protagonist's own conscience.

- Against an illness.
- Between alternative loyalties, ideologies or ambitions.
- Just an argument between two protagonists . . .

and any number of other variations.

Whereas a short story will usually describe the resolution of just one problem, a novel needs many problems and many obstacles. Let there be a number of crises in your story: let each crisis be more serious – more difficult to resolve – than its predecessor; let the climax of the whole story be the overcoming of the biggest crisis of all. Think of the ever-mounting crises in your storyline as a graph with peaks and troughs – successive peaks and troughs being higher than the ones before.

Strip down a model

Now, a potentially extremely valuable pre-start exercise. You have already decided on the genre within which you will be writing. And you will/should have read a lot of successful books in this genre. Now select the book you liked best and pull it to pieces. Strip it down.

1. Write a brief (about 200 words) description of each of the leading characters. Take note of where in the book you became aware of their characteristics – the reader is seldom given too much early on. Also pay particular attention to *how* you are given the information. Sometimes you are not told at all, but the character is so alive that, almost without realising it, you have filled in the gaps from your own imagination.
2. In note form, write a summary of the contents of each chapter, paying particular attention to the number of separate scenes per chapter. Effectively, write a chapter-by-chapter synopsis of the book – get back to what the writer could have worked from.
3. Note the positioning and magnitude of every climax and

      crisis (and/or love scene); notice the 'hooks' and 'cliff-hangers' at chapter starts and ends. Maybe draw yourself a graph of the increasing suspense which the novelist has generated – in all types of book, not just in thrillers.

4.   Investigate the *amount* of dialogue, the *amount* of description (and how 'flowery' it is – or isn't), and the *amount* of action in the story. When I did this exercise I found it helped to take a paperback novel and highlight each 'element' – dialogue, description and action – in different colours throughout. The first time I did it, I got quite a surprise. In Technicolor.

5.   Take note also of the general lengths of speeches, sentences, paragraphs. In genre novels these are usually fairly short. Look at *how* the dialogue is punctuated. More details on dialogue in the next chapter.

You are going to model your own novel along more-or-less the same lines as the one you have pulled to pieces. Don't copy slavishly, but do try to follow the way your model has gone. Remember: your model got published: that's your objective too.

The synopsis

You have your idea, your characters are alive in your mind, and you know where, and, of course, when, the action of your story is to take place. You have thought of a number of worsening crises and how your characters will resolve them; you know the general plot, the basic storyline. And you have written it down – for fear of losing it. At this stage, the plot/storyline should fit comfortably onto a single A4 page of typescript. (You will also have a well-filled sheet of notes about each of the characters and lots of hastily scribbled ideas for scenes and sub-plots to fit into the story. For each leading character in your novel, write a brief life-story – 300 words or so. But also have a look at the next chapter – on characters.

    Now the detailed synopsis. This is where you convert and expand your storyline, complete with peaks and troughs, into individual chapter contents. Let us assume – and you must determine this for yourself, from your up-to-date market study of other books in your chosen genre – that your book is to be 60,000 words long, in fifteen chapters. Thus, the chapters will each be about 4,000 words long. You need to pack enough action into the synopsis of each chapter to let you write 4,000 words from it. Keep that 4,000-word thought in mind all the while you are writing the synopsis.

With your storyline in front of you, make notes of the content of each of the (fifteen) chapters. You might write a hundred of so words of notes about each chapter. Pick up all of the major scenes you have already identified in your storyline. Build in the major, and worsening, crises you have planned.

And the chances are that you will find that you still haven't got enough material to fill all the chapters in the book.

Cliff-hangers

Maybe you need another sub-plot; maybe you haven't put enough obstacles in the way of the lead character(s); maybe you aren't reckoning on 'milking' each scene to the limit? Developing your storyline into the more detailed synopsis is where the art/craft/knack of storytelling begins to come in. And don't forget the need for a cliff-hanger at the end of each chapter and a hook at the start of the next. You've got to keep them turning the pages.

Think of the late-night reader, knowing that she really ought to turn out the light and go to sleep. 'At the end of this chapter,' she vows. It's your job as a novelist to stop this: your story must be 'un-put-down-able'.

There are two schools of thought about synopses. Many writers don't plan ahead as comprehensively as I have recommended here. Some extremely fine – and successful – writers never prepare a synopsis at all. If you ask them how they write, they will tell you, in all honesty, that they start by simply knowing their characters well, and then letting the story develop. Sometimes they know what the ending is going to be but seldom how their characters are to get there.

From my own, admittedly somewhat limited, fiction-writing experience, I cannot understand that approach at all. Clearly, though, it works for some. Maybe their conscious mind does not know the storyline but their subconscious mind does?

For the beginning writer, writing within a genre frame-work, I recommend using a carefully worked-out synopsis. Not to do that would be like starting to build a house without a floor plan. The resultant shape will be higgledy-piggledy, the foundations incomplete, the supports misplaced and the construction unsupervisable. Despite the best quality materials, it is bound to end up a poor job overall. I'd sooner trust an architect than my subconscious.

Checking the synopsis

When you have completed your synopsis, check it. Make sure that all of the sub-plots are properly ended, that there are no loose ends. Make sure that the essential clues – to later events – are in their right places. Make sure that you have actually used – followed up on – all the planted clues. Make sure that all the characters are introduced at the right spot in the story. You can't say, in Chapter 15, 'Oh, I forgot to tell you – Fanny had a younger sister...'

Think about the opening of your story. Are you starting *late* enough, with a real bang? You can always bring in the 'back-story' by using a flashback – refer back to Chapter 7 for this.

With a short story, I suggested that you should aim at grabbing the reader's attention within the first couple of sentences. You get a little longer in a novel. If necessary, you can have the first two to three hundred words. Your opening has got to be really good; it is always one of the most difficult parts of a novel to write; it is often sensible to go back and completely rewrite your original opening once the rest of the story is complete.

The first few pages of a novel should:

- Introduce the leading character and just possibly some of the other protagonists. The reader needs to get to know the lead character as soon as possible, in order to identify with him/her.
- Identify the tone/nature of the book. The reader needs to be assured that the book is indeed the straightforward SF/romance/Western that the cover and title suggest.
- Capture the reader's attention so that the book cannot now be put down. The opening can be during, or the immediate aftermath of, a conflict; ideally, it sets the scene for the whole book.

Viewpoint

But back to the synopsis. Have you chosen the right lead character(s)? Think about the main viewpoint. Is the novel this person's story?

Whereas a short story should almost always be told from a single (third person) viewpoint, a novel is less restrictive. You can tell your story from a number of different viewpoints. This eases the constraint imposed by the single viewpoint – but don't go mad and use too many viewpoints. Keep the number of viewpoint characters down. And make sure that it is always clear whose viewpoint is now being used: make the changeover explicit – maybe by a break in the story.

Research

So far, all the plotting, the preparation, has come from your imagination. But your actual writing has got to be correct.

If your hero leaves London bound for Scotland, driving on the M3 motorway, he'll take an awful long time getting there. The M3 would take him to a Channel port on the south coast. This would bring your thrilling novel to an unexpected close – and your credibility would be zero.

If you want to write about someone who travelled to China

with Marco Polo, you've got to get your dates right. If your heroine serves a candlelit dinner for her hero, you need to allow her enough time – and the right sort of onions (shallots) – to prepare and cook the *boeuf bourguignon*. And she certainly shouldn't open a 'bottle of red Sauternes wine' to go with it – Sauternes is a sweet white wine which goes with puddings. All this correctness entails research.

No, don't panic. You don't have to go (back) to college or university before you write your novel. But, as in article writing, you do have to:

Know your subject well before writing about it.

And that means not merely your imaginary subjects, your characters and their actions, but also, particularly, the setting.

If you are going to write a family saga about a brewery business, for instance, you must investigate first. You might want to describe how beers were brewed in the nineteenth century and then how they are brewed today. You should read one or two books about early brewing techniques. (You don't need to become an expert, just get to understand, so that you don't make a fool of yourself when describing the process.)

Equally important, and potentially more fun, you could approach your local brewery for information. Explain to the Press Officer that you are about to write a book about an old brewing family and would much appreciate a guided tour of the brewery to see how up-to-date techniques are applied.

It would probably be wise to research the early brewing techniques before your visit, so that any questions you ask are suitably knowledgeable. And while you're there, sow the seed of future contacts too: you will almost certainly need to do more research while you're writing. You don't always know what facts you need until you're in mid-story.

Many writers become totally absorbed in the research, which can be enjoyable and fascinating. If this is you, stop. Remind yourself that you are a writer, not a researcher. You need only find out enough to colour your background. In a novel, the story's the thing, not the facts.

No matter how much research you do for your novel, it is essential that it doesn't show through too much in your writing. Don't incorporate large chunks of information straight out of the reference book. One good way of using your research is for your character to discover whatever it is you want to include. Even better, let the character actually carry out the process you have researched – mash, sparge and boil the grain, or whatever is done before adding the hops. But not in too much detail.

An American writer explained it rather well. Paraphrased for the benefit of the pure-minded, he said something like, 'Research is like manure: a little of it, spread thinly, does wonders, but in large dollops, no thanks.'

But research should not be a problem. For modern novels maybe all you need is a travel book of the country and a map of the main town. For a period romance – if you are careful about how much background detail you include – a children's history book or an encyclopaedia could well suffice. For a thriller, the shoulder insignias and titles of rank in the Lusitanian security police may be all you need to know.

The important thing about research is:

If you give details or facts – make sure they're correct.

You can be sure that if you include something – however unimportant – in your story . . . and get it wrong, someone will notice. And that someone will always write to your publisher and tell him so.

Keep a record of the sources of all your research – including, as appropriate, reference book title and page number.

Basic reference books

Almost irrespective of what you write, reference books dealing with general subjects are useful to most writers. Don't spend a fortune on this personal reference library – paperback and second-hand books will do fine. Of course, don't forget the wonders of the Internet, Google and the Wikipedia. But some personal reference books are a wise resource too. I suggest:

● A really good English dictionary. Don't rely solely on the dictionary in your word processor.

- A single-volume encyclopaedia. I have, as my 'first reference source', the excellent Penguin paperback one.
- Where appropriate, one or two basic history books dealing with the country about which you intend to write. If you are going to mention it, or have any action taking place during it, you really do have to be sure of the dates of, e.g. the Korean War.
- If you propose to write novels with a historical flavour, you need to know about the clothes and styles of the period – few Chinese women now have bound feet, few men pigtails. There are histories of costume.
- A book of dates – I have the Penguin *Chronology of the Modern World*.
- A book of names – one elementary source of English language first names and their European counterparts is a twelve-page appendix to the tiny *Collins Gem Thesaurus*. That has always been sufficient for my needs.
- One or more Dictionaries of Quotations. These are good for thinking up novel-titles – and sometimes even ideas for new stories.
- Simple books about other interests which impinge on your novel-writing activities. Children's books are often ideal.

Writing and rewriting

All right, now you're ready to go. You can get down to the actual writing of your novel.

There are two schools of thought about how to go about that too. One faction suggests that you sweat over each page or two, perfecting them before you move on to the next – and then never change it when it's all complete. The other faction suggests that you should just keep going – writing from the synopsis – until you get to the end; then go back to the beginning and rewrite/edit/polish the whole.

My own preference is half-way between the two. I write fairly fast. All the while I'm writing, I struggle to find the right word or phrase. Using a word processor, I also frequently go back within the chapter I'm working on and change, or add, an explanation, or some dialogue. As I start up again next day, I re-read the previous day's work – to get back 'into the swing' – and inevitably revise it a little more. Then, at the end of each chapter, I re-read a draft copy of the typescript – it looks different on paper from what it did on the screen – and again revise and polish it. Finally, when the book is complete, I re-read the whole, correcting, editing and polishing for the last time. Then I print it all out and send it off.

However you do it, the editing, polishing and rewriting is perhaps the most important task in producing your novel. Skimp it at your peril. At this stage too, it is wise to check, once again, what you have written, against your research sources.

One final word of advice. Write something – even just a hundred words if you're pushed for time – of your novel every day without fail. If you miss many days the characters may no longer be alive and kicking inside your head. It could take quite a while to resuscitate them and you might never achieve it.

Children's novels

If your ambition is to write novels for children, virtually all the above advice will be equally applicable. You need a really good storyline with lots of conflict, well-rounded and believably 'live' characters, and a powerful build-up of tension/suspense. And I wouldn't dream of writing without a detailed synopsis. One major difference – most children's books are shorter.

Novels for teenagers can be 'stand-alone' books of virtually any length from about 40,000 words up. Books for 9- to 12-year-olds are frequently 'stand-alones' and tend to be in the 20,000 to 40,000 word range. Books for 5- to 9-year-olds are often the best target for the beginning writer, they are usually within publishers' series and can be anything from 1,000 to 10,000 words long. You must check the individual series requirements. Picture-books are very short – usually between about 200 and 1,000 words long – and possibly the hardest of all to write.

The generally shorter length of all children's books doesn't make them any easier to write. Children are demanding readers. They usually know what they want, and expect to get it.

Children expect plenty of action in their stories. They want to identify with the main characters in the books. Child characters can be a bit naughty – like Richmal Crompton's William for instance – but deep down, well-meaning. They welcome – and if you can manage it, the more the better – humour of all sorts: slapstick, simple word puns, making fools of grown-ups . . . you name it.

One thing you must never do in writing for children is write down to them. Use fairly simple words (although an occasional 'hard' word is no bad idea) and an easy writing style, yes; provide a straightforward, not-too-complicated plot, yes; with extra-bad 'baddies' and extra-good 'goodies', yes, maybe; but a patronising attitude, never. **Write for the child in yourself.** And if there isn't one there, don't.

Another important qualification for writing for children – exactly as recommended above for writing within the main adult genres – is that you must *like* reading such stories. If you think of writing for children as just an easy way to get published, you'll fail. And deservedly so.

Chapter 9:

Characters and Dialogue

Apart from the actual storyline – developed from the idea/theme and showing how the characters react to conflicts of some form or another – the essentials of any work of fiction are characters and dialogue. Indeed, you cannot properly develop a storyline without the characters, as we have seen. And characters who don't talk to each other are less than alive.

So before you can write your novel – genre, 'straight' or children's, it makes no difference – you need to create the characters. Yes, create.

Creating characters

How do you go about creating characters? Non-writers will often ask whether you 'put yourself' into your novel(s). Writers of steamy romances are most likely to be on the receiving end of such queries; the classic response is that Agatha Christie didn't have to be a murderess to write whodunits.

In another sense though, every character in every story you write is you – they come alive thinking your thoughts, feeling your feelings, wishing, and maybe fulfilling, your wishes. But only partly. Your characters must not be wholly or solely you, or you'll soon find you can't create any more. You'll have 'written yourself out' – a 'one-book wonder'.

Nor do you create fictional characters by taking someone you know and just giving them a new name. Even if you do decide to write a story based on, or about, your friend Joe Hackenbacker, you will soon find out you don't really know

Joe. You only know the outward Joe; you don't know the Joe who Joe himself thinks he is.

To write about Joe you will need to know the whole Joe – so you will have to fill in the gaps. Maybe you start by basing Bill – your renamed character – on Joe. Then, running out of knowledge, you base another aspect of Bill's personality on a tetchy old aunt of yours. Later still, you want a characteristic turn of phrase for Bill – and you take that from someone else you know.

Bill is no longer Joe: he has become your own creation – a deliberate mélange of your acquaintances, experiences and ideas. And you will probably know more about Bill than you will ever know about any person in real life.

In practice, your characters will often be even more diverse than Bill. You will seldom start from a specific real-life individual.

One way – toss a coin

The American novelist Dick Winfield suggests a way of fabricating a believable character out of thin air. He needs a minor Aunt Tilly character. He decides what she is like by playing chance, and by answering questions on the toss of a coin:

Age:	Write the numbers from 40 to 60 on scraps of paper, put them in a hat and draw one out.
Widow or spinster:	Toss a coin: heads = widow, tails = spinster.
Beautiful or ugly:	Toss a coin.
Intellectual or 'fluff':	Toss a coin

. . . and so on.

Continue asking questions and tossing the coin until Aunt Tilly is filled out and comes alive. And . . . if you don't like the coin result – toss it again. You're in charge; the coin is merely an aid.

Winfield goes on to recommend that the budding novelist next writes a brief no-holds-barred description of Aunt Tilly, as if writing to a friend about her. You must also think or decide whether jet planes were around when Aunt Tilly was born; whether there was a war on when she was at primary school; what sort of music she grew up with – jazz, swing, Sinatra, Blur or rap; and what sort of boys she dated. All these things will influence the way she – and similarly, any of the other characters – will think and act.

Describing your characters

Most of us, when we start to describe someone, think in terms of generalities. It is polite, socially more acceptable, to say that a person is 'somewhat out of step with modern attitudes'. But what does this really mean? Only you know the attitudes of the rest of your created characters, and thus the 'norm'.

You must be more specific in your thoughts. Your character will more readily come alive if you say, 'He's so old-fashioned – he won't even go to a lady doctor!' Or, 'He hasn't spoken to his daughter since he heard that she was living with a bloke.'

Add these characteristics to your mini-biography of each of your characters (see Fig. 4). And don't forget the 'warts' we mentioned in Chapter 7.

When you come to write the book itself, you will have that biography in front of you – and fixed firmly in your mind too. But you won't merely repeat the description in the book: drip-feed your readers. Give them only a little of Aunt Tilly, at a time.

Jo	
Name:	Joanne – known as Jo – Kilter.
Age:	Coming up to ten (birthday 6 June, therefore star-sign Gemini).
Friends:	Only Tony – and Duke (a mouse, Tony's 'familiar').
Parents:	Dad, Peter Kilter, professional footballer – plays for Belwether United and England. (He is kidnapped in *The Wiz-kid and the Football Caper.*)
	Mum: 'Round' and jolly. Always 'there' – at home, usually in kitchen, cooking.
House:	Nice mid-price-range 3-bedroom detached house; large garden at rear with alleyway over the back garden fence. The estate is a pleasant 1960s one on opposite (better) side of Belwether from Tony's. Road name not specified.
Personality:	Decidedly tom-boyish, almost always cheerful – looks on bright side. Adventurous. Talkative/chatty.
Appearance:	Slightly freckled face; long, mousey-coloured hair, beyond her shoulders, usually tied up with elastic band in pony-tail. Big blue eyes. 'Normal' clothes – jeans and sweaters, seldom a dress. Average height for age, not skinny – just 'ordinary'.
School:	The nearby local primary school – not the one Tony goes to, on other side of town. She is bright, usually near top of class – but not 'bookish', just clever.
Interests:	Mad about football (naturally – see Dad) and bike-riding . . . and having adventures with the Wiz-kid. And she absolutely LOVES flying with Tony.
Food likes:	Like Tony, she adores bread pudding. Likes most other foods too – preferably in abundance. And, of course, crisps, chocolate bars, and pop-corn.

Fig. 4. An example of an author's brief notes about a character. This is Jo, the best friend of Tony Bright, the Wiz-kid. She appears in all the Wiz-kid books after the first.

Early on, tell the reader enough to visualise the character more-or-less correctly – so that he/she doesn't imagine wrongly and get annoyed when you release more details – but not so much that there is nothing left to imagine. By all means tell the reader that the character is unattractive/ugly but you don't have to describe the glass eye, the hare-lip or the mole on the chin in clinical detail unless it is central to the story.

Names

Think too about the names of your characters. Re-read the relevant section of Chapter 7. Names are just as important – or more so – in a novel as they are in a short story. And, whereas in a short story, the name can – if necessary – be unusual and difficult to pronounce, this is unwise in a novel where it is used again and again.

Names are a particular problem in writing in the science fiction genre. How would you pronounce Raztupisp-minz (yes, really!), a character in Niven and Pournelle's *Footfall*? Yes, I know, you *can* pronounce it – slowly, once. But to keep on 'thinking' it as you read? No way. I 'thought' 'Raz-t'. And is it a male or female character? If you can't feel the name in your head while reading the book, it's hard to identify with it. I *still* lie awake nights worrying over whether Anne McCaffrey's Menolly – in *Dragonsong* and one of my all-time favourite characters – is MENolly or MenOLLy.

In any sort of story, take care in your choice of names. It can be confusing if you have two characters in the same story with similar names: avoid mixing Lacey with Tracey; don't let Christopher fall in love with Christine; stop Jimmy Walls working in an office for a boss called Wells. Equally, don't go in for too many exotic-sounding (or cribbed-from-TV-soaps) names; one or two are enough for any book.

If you can't think of sensible-sounding last names, investigate ancient gravestones in your local cemetery or, better, a map or gazetteer of towns and villages. Beware too much alliteration in first and last names – Jimmy James sounds like a nickname. Mum and Dad James are more likely to have named him Richard or Thomas.

Watch out for the problem of using a real person's unusual name though: the classic disclaimer, '... any resemblance to living persons is purely coincidental,' has little legal value.

But names apart, perhaps the most important way in which you can bring characters properly to life is by their speech.

Recognisable speech

Some people speak well, others less so. Some people talk a lot, others are taciturn. Some people use long words and speak in a pompous manner, seeking unsuccessfully to impress; others speak clearly and simply – and automatically impress.

Each of your characters should have his or her own identifiable way of speaking. One definition of a bunch of well-rounded, believable characters is that, even without 'John said, Jane said' attributions, they are readily identifiable.

Do not, though, attempt to capture regional and other dialects phonetically on paper. If you drop every H when committing a person's speech to paper, your book will not be an easy read. Just omit one occasionally and use conventional English thereafter. Include the occasional 'Och Aye' (or suchlike) if you must, to emphasise a character's Scottish ancestry – and leave it at that.

If the character is speaking in a language other than English, try to convey the *feel* of the foreign language *structure* rather than by using actual foreign words. And do it only enough for the accent, language, or whatever to be identifiable. Then leave it to the reader's imagination.

Real life or fictional dialogue?

As above, characters come alive from the dialogue you put into their mouths (or hear them saying, in your mind). And the more realistic your dialogue, the more realistic your characters. Well . . . er . . . well, not quite. Fictional dialogue has to be better than real-life dialogue.

Imagine recording all the conversation going on around you, in your home and office, throughout the day. You could actually record it. It's easier to let my imagination do it for you.

At home, the first conversation of the day might go something like this:

'G'morning.'

'Oo-oo-ugh-er. Whassa-time? Have I gotta get up?'

'You'll be late for work if you don't.'

'My mouth tastes like the bottom of a bird cage. Why didn't you stop me from having that fourth dr . . .'

'Ugh, you're so revolting. Serves you right. Get up!'

'Slave-driver. Is the coffee on?'

'Yes, and getting colder all the while you . . .'

'All right, all right. I'm coming.'

Later perhaps the conversation might be like this:

'You're driving much too fast.'

'Oh, for Pete's sake, stop nagging.'

'Watch that kid!'

'Stupid little so-and-so.'

'You'll be on time tonight, won't you? I'm going to Keep Fit.'

'What, again? I might have to work late. I thought . . .'

'Why shouldn't I? It's fun. There are some real nice blokes there too. Why don't you ...?'

'Don't be daft.'

'All right. I'll get Bill to ...'

'Don't you dare. I'll be on time.'

At work, the non-work conversation will be something like this:

'Did you see that old *Bond* movie on the box last night?'

'Yeah. Terrific, wasn't it? Specially that bit when those two girls ...'

'Yeah, that was really good wasn't it? And then when he ...'

'And, cor! Those ...'

Boring, isn't it? All of it. Sorry! But so much of our everyday conversation is just like that. Yes, all of us, we're all as bad. Maybe different words, different interests, but always boring. Trivial matters discussed in a mundane fashion. If you put all (or even any) of that in your story, it would never take off – and would inevitably be rejected. The conversation does not carry the story forward, nor does it even tell us much about the characters. They bicker a lot, so they're probably a married couple. But that's all we've learned.

Fictional dialogue has to sound realistic, while at the same time being far better, and always moving the story along. There is no room for trivial chit-chat in fiction. Fictional dialogue has to provide snippets of extra information that cannot be conveyed in any other way and must illuminate the personality of each character.

Rules for dialogue

A few simple rules for writing good fictional dialogue:

- Try to ensure that conflict is somehow involved in, implied by, or in the background of every speech.

- Ensure that the characters do not 'come across' as trite, merely mouthing clichés and everyday trivia. Make sure they have something important or useful to say – or keep them quiet.

- Check that the words and phrases said by your characters are as cleverly 'turned', without appearing too clever, and as colourful as possible. Equally, let the words be 'in character' – and preferably identifiably unique – to the character speaking.

- Never *tell* your reader that a character is witty, or sly, or clever. *Show* the reader this characteristic through the words that the character uses. Let him/her say something witty, sly or clever. Or show by an action.

Throughout all your fictional writing – not just dialogue – that last point is a really Golden rule. So let's emphasise it:
Show, don't tell.
Fig. 5 (opposite) illustrates this point.
The 'tell' example is dull and reads like a news report. The 'show' example is... *alive*, and tells the reader something about the characters.

Tell

Later that day, Inspector Donavan sent a woman PC round to the family's house. She told the mother that the police had found the body of a young girl who they thought was probably her daughter. They needed her to come to the police station morgue as soon as possible to make an identification. The mother was, of course, very upset. The woman PC consoled her as best she could but she knew it wasn't enough.

Show

As she walked up the path to the Wilsons' house, Polly was worried. She recognised that, right now, the Inspector couldn't make time to pass on the bad news to the missing girl's family. But it was an awful job he'd landed her with.

'Mrs Wilson?' she enquired, 'Can I come in?'

The dowdy-looking woman who had answered the door stood aside. Polly eased past her into a neat little hallway with a flowery carpet that had seen better days. The other woman gestured that Polly should go through the door on the left. She followed her in.

'I'm awfully sorry, Mrs Wilson, but we have found . . .'

'NO!' Jane's mother shrieked.

'We're not at all sure that it's Jane, Mrs Wilson, but we have found a body in Witsend Wood. It's a young girl of about the same age as Jane. We would like you to come and see. You will be able to tell us for sure, whether it's Jane.'

Mrs Wilson leant forward and rested her head on her hands. Her whole body shook in anguish. Polly moved closer and pulled her gently towards her.

'I'll take you there now, if you like, Mrs Wilson . . .'

'Please – and stay with me.'

'Of course . . .'

Fig. 5. An example of 'Show, don't tell'.

Now back to the simple, basic rules of dialogue:

- Don't let your speeches go on for too long. Keep sentences and speeches short – bouncing to and fro like a tennis ball. Remember too that, in real life, people interrupt. In a lively conversation, people are seldom allowed to finish a long rambling pontification. (Not if I'm around, anyway.) Let this happen in your fiction – but not too often or it can be irritating. Some find it so in real life too.

- In dialogue, use the abbreviated forms of words which are common in speech but perhaps less often used in more formal text. I have to phrase that advice carefully, as I often use such abbreviated forms in my writing, to lighten up my style when offering advice/tuition.

  As an example, you could well write, 'Tom did not feel at all well'. Within dialogue however, Jane talking to her mother, for example, would be more likely to say, 'Tom didn't feel at all well.' If Jane had used the unabbreviated form, it would imply an unintended emphasis, 'Tom did *not* feel at all well.'

- Avoid qualifying the dialogue attribution unnecessarily. 'He said' or 'She said' are perfectly adequate most of the time. It should seldom be necessary to write, 'He said, angrily.' The state of mind should be obvious from the spoken words and/or the surrounding 'atmosphere'. Again, show, don't tell. It might, though, be helpful to write, 'She murmured' or 'She whispered', if there is no other way of indicating the quietness of the speech.

  Avoid seeking too many variations on the simple, 'he said/she said' attribution. You seldom need to use: replied, muttered, explained, argued, shouted, responded. Occasionally, perhaps; frequently, and it looks amateurish.

Readers don't actually notice the 'he said/she said' attributions; their eyes ignore them, they become 'part of the furniture'. Indeed, you can write quite long exchanges of dialogue with only occasional attribution. The speaker should be clear from the way of speaking and the views propounded. Anyway, so long as the dialogue is bouncing back and forth in order, the reader will retain a grasp of who is saying what. In a good 'bouncing ball' conversation you need only add in a 'he said/she said' attribution about every half-dozen or so short speeches.

An alternative to direct attribution is to link the occasional speech to a named action, e.g. ' "Not tonight, Josephine." Leon shook his head as he backed away.'

Layout of dialogue

Many beginners experience difficulty with the punctuation and layout of dialogue. This suggests that they don't look closely enough at published fiction. They need only copy the punctuation used and the layout favoured in published work to get it right. But, for convenience, let's spell it out:

- Start a fresh (indented) paragraph for each new speech – i.e. by each new person – no matter how brief the 'speech', even just a couple of words. If, however, the same person continues speaking after a pause during which you describe what he/she is doing, the second speech can – but doesn't have to – be within the same paragraph. Thus:

  'I'm sure he'll ring soon,' said Tony. He turned towards the windows. The night was drawing in. It was turning colder and he had noticed that Sally was shivering. He closed the window and pulled the curtains together. Suddenly the room felt smaller, more cosy. 'If anything had happened, we'd have heard by now.'

- Put all speech in quotes. Depending on the convention adopted by the publisher/editor, the quote marks can be single or double inverted commas. The use of single quote marks for dialogue is fairly common usage today. The really important thing is that you should be consistent – use either single or double quote marks throughout.

- If – and don't let it happen too often – a character makes a longer-than-usual speech, running on beyond the extent of a single paragraph, don't close the quotes at the end of the first paragraph. Start the new/second paragraph with quotes though, and when the speech ends, close the quotes.

- You should usually separate speech from attribution by a comma. For example:

'John ought to have got there by now,' said Sally.

Or:

Sally was worried. She said, 'John ought to have got there by now.'

And when a single-sentence speech is broken by the attribution, you should again use commas, both before and after. Thus:

'Yes,' said Sally, 'but he ought to have got there by now.'

Notice that the second part of the one-sentence speech is not graced with a capital B.

- Rather than include unbroken over-long speeches – the multi-paragraph ones referred to already – it is often helpful to insert a bit of description or action. Not quite the same as the double-speech within one paragraph illustrated above – more like this:

'. . . So you really don't need to worry, my dear.' Tony walked across the room and took Sally's hand. 'I'm sure he's all right, Sally. He's only been gone a few minutes.'

Or even slip in an occasional tiny interruption:

'. . . a whole lot of things he had to do. And he's only been gone a few . . .'

'Yes, Tony, but . . .'

'Please don't interrupt me, Sally. I'm coming to that . . . and he would certainly have wanted to clear up before he left.'

And that little interruption illustrated Tony's pompous personality rather well. Another example of 'Show, don't tell'.

Straightforward, isn't it? And, remember, it is through dialogue that your characters come to life. Work hard at your dialogue.

Chapter 10:

Writing a Non-fiction Book

Every year, at least four or five times as many non-fiction books as novels are published in Britain. You will therefore have four or five times as many chances of getting a non-fiction book published, than if you were to write a novel. It may not sell as many copies as a best-selling novel – but not all novels are best-sellers.

There are other advantages in writing a non-fiction book. Most beginner-writers yearn to write a novel; so there are fewer would-be non-fiction writers – so the competition is less. Again, you have more chances.

Your novel, if for adult readers, will usually need to be at least 70,000 words long. Many non-fiction books – like this one – are not much more than 40,000 words. So, another plus-point – you have to write less to get published.

Perhaps the best thing about writing a non-fiction book, though, is that you get it approved before you write it. With a first novel, you have to complete it before a publisher will consider it. With a non-fiction book, you sell it before you write it. Well, before you write much of it.

A non-fiction author offers publishers a book proposal: a detailed synopsis and usually one or two sample chapters. A publisher likes the idea. The author and the publisher discuss, amend and agree on the proposed content; the publisher checks the author's 'subject credentials' and writing style; and the project is agreed. The 'credentials' are not necessarily academic. Rather, the publisher needs assurance that the author is an appropriately knowledgeable person to write about the subject. A contract is signed; the publisher agrees to pay the author an advance; the author goes off and writes the book – *knowing* that it will be published.

If you know a lot about almost any subject, you can write a non-fiction book about it. And probably get it published.

Money

You won't necessarily make a lot of money from your non-fiction book. You certainly won't make as much as the author of a real block-busting best-selling novel. But you could well make more money than many a 'first novelist', a lot of whom sink without trace.

Novels are usually first published in Britain in hard covers – and seldom sell more than a thousand or so copies, mainly to libraries. (It is only when novels go into paperback that they make really big money.) Many non-fiction books go directly into paperback; most can expect to sell a couple of thousand copies – and many keep on selling for several years. In total, spread over time, the average non-fiction book will usually earn more than the average first novel.

A book about what?

Let's consider non-fiction book subjects. Non-fiction books include:

- Biographies and autobiographies (memoirs) – including the 'life stories' of pop groups and other celebrities.
- History books – including the 'just yesterday' history, of football teams and the like; of major crimes as well as 'real' history.
- Self-help books – vaguely (or very) philosophical books, covering everything from gaining self-assurance to enjoying better sex.
- Instructional books – teaching about everything, from writing to house-building, from staff interviewing to better sex (again), and about all sorts of jobs, crafts and hobbies.

- Encyclopaedias – and lesser 'all about' books – including books about Chinese porcelain, English dragons, heraldry, and the American wart-hog, for example.
- Textbooks – anything from primary school books to postgraduate monographs.

Biographies and autobiographies

Many budding non-fiction authors think of writing their memoirs. Every time a general or a leading politician retires, we are told that he intends to write his memoirs. Luckily, they don't all get finished.

Unless . . .

a)   You are very well-known – like a President, or a fashion model, or a pop mega-star.

b)   You have done something really spectacular – like swimming the Atlantic with one arm tied behind your back, or you've visited the moon – twice . . .

Don't.

The market for the story of your (ordinary) life is small – you will probably be wasting your time even preparing a synopsis. You might be more successful writing a biography of someone else – someone from the past. The snag here is that most 'heavy' biographies are written by academics. If you are close to an established star personality, you might be able to write the story of his or her life. If you are not already close though, don't. Publishers are more likely to commission an established writer than consider a book by an unknown.

Memoirs

But, you say, money isn't everything. You really do want to write your memoirs. And you accept that these will not be for publication, but rather, for your children and their children's children to read in later years. That's fine – it's a great thing to do. Just don't go about it casually: approach it in a professional manner.

Approach the writing of the story of your life as you would the writing of a novel (i.e. not as a non-fiction book): plan out what you are going to say, write a preliminary synopsis, identify – if not major conflicts and crises – high and low points and really 'write your heart out' about such events.

Ensure that your descendants will actually enjoy reading the story of your life. An ancestor cannot expect a captive readership any more than any other writer. You must earn it. Make the story of your life really interesting and, if possible, entertaining. Just don't expect to sell it.

History books

Unless you are a professional historian, or a well-established author, many of the obstacles in the way of writing biographies will also make history a difficult subject for a book. A publisher will want to know your 'credentials' for writing such a book. And usually an academic will be better qualified than an ordinary writer. Not all academics are good writers though – they just know their subject well. When you are an experienced writer, this fact may just 'let you in'.

Academics, of course, have no 'edge' when it comes to writing about major crimes, nostalgia, or the history of a famous football team. One of these days, if you have the right contacts, you may be able to persuade a publisher that you are the person to write that book. But as a first book – most unlikely.

Better prospects

It is in one or other of the remaining non-fiction book classes that the beginning writer will have the best prospects. If you have learned something interesting or useful, by your own experience – such as how to come to terms with bereavement, divorce, or redundancy – you can write a book about it. If you are skilled at your job, craft or hobby – anything from lace-making to personnel management – you can write a book about it. If you are a 'mini-expert' on almost anything – a collector of Pacific Ocean sea-shells, of Dresden figurines, or you know a lot about dragons, perhaps – you can write a book about it. And if you are a teacher, at any level from primary school to university, you can perhaps write a textbook.

Those are the best areas in which to start writing non-fiction. Henceforth we will concentrate on how to write this type of book.

As an example, let's say we are going to write about Widget Collecting. The approach would be exactly the same were your subject to be 'How to Write Short Stories', 'Conquering Your Fear of Spiders', or 'Esperanto for Primary Schools'.

Who will buy it?

First, think about the possible market for such a book. Is widget collecting a popular activity or are widgets as rare as green dogs and their collectors even rarer? If the latter, you and your ever-loving mother are the only likely buyers of your proposed book. That's not a big enough market to make the book publishable. So think again.

But let's be more optimistic. Widget collecting is the new *thing*. There are lots of widgets to be picked up at car-boot sales, and there is much interest in them. And you have one of the world's best collections of widgets.

Not only have you a fine collection but, because of your long-standing interest, you have researched the history of widget making in a number of different countries. It begins to sound like a worthwhile subject for a book.

The competition

From where did you gather all your knowledge about widgets? From books? Are those books still in print? Are there already lots of books about widget collecting? If so, why should anyone be interested in a new book?

Again, we are lucky. There have only been a couple of new books on widget collecting in the last few years. All the other books on the subject are much older. You rummaged through innumerable second-hand bookshops to find them.

You need to do more checking though. Call at your local library and look up widgets in the non-fiction subject index. Investigate all the widget books it lists. Ask the librarian whether there are any more books on the subject – or if there are any new widget books in the pipeline. Librarians enjoy providing this sort of help.

Make your book different

Review the two 'recent' books on widget collecting. How can you make your book different? Maybe one of the books is very academic and theoretical; you could certainly make yours more practical and down to earth.

The other current book may be very good. But you don't like the way it is written or set out; it may look more boring than it really is. You can make your book better-looking and easier to understand. Or maybe you can restrict your book to the collecting of cheaper widgets – that would attract a wider readership.

The final piece of initial research now. Are there any magazines dealing with widget collecting? If it doesn't have its own specialist magazine, is the subject dealt with regularly in other collectors' magazines? Does widget collecting feature in their small ads? Are there shops specialising in antique widgets? The answers to these questions will begin to give you an idea of the interest in widget collecting. You will need this information to convince a publisher that there is a market for your book.

What to include

Your next job is to think about the book itself. Think about what you are going to put in it.

Take a blank sheet of paper and head it WIDGETS. (You

must spend time trying to think up a catchy, yet descriptive title. Keep it short. Again, as with fiction – *the title is vital*.)

The next part is hard grind. What are you going to say/ write about widgets? (Why on earth did you start off on this exercise?)

Try listing what you know about widgets:

- You know about the prices of different widgets, which ones are bargains and which are over-priced.
- You know how and where widgets are made.
- You know the history of widget development.
- You know a bit about foreign widgets. (Can you find out more? Do you need to?)
- You know how best to start a collection, where to pick up good cheap widgets.
- You know what widgets are used for, and how.

You may need more than that for a book, so dig a bit deeper into your memory. Ah yes . . .

- You know the history of the designer of the British widget, John Smith.

Look back at that list. Those different aspects would surely make a reasonable set of chapter headings – and that is what you are initially working towards.

You have listed all of the aspects of widget collecting that you can think of. Now you must ensure that you have really covered all possible areas. You may need to broaden your own knowledge, by research, in order to cover the subject fully.

Go back to the two recent books on widget collecting. Compare their chapter headings with your ideas. Do they cover a broader field than you? Shouldn't you too include the aspects they have but you don't? You may decide not to follow them in their coverage – but you must be able to justify that decision. And not wanting to bother with the extra research is no answer.

A logical sequence

If you are now satisfied that your coverage of the subject is correct, sort your chapter ideas into a logical sequence. At the same time, think up short – three or four word – chapter titles. Maybe you end up with the following chapter titles and sequence:

1. What are widgets?
2. Why collect widgets?
3. The widget story.
4. John Smith – widget-maker.
5. How widgets are made.
6. Foreign widgets.
7. Starting your widget collection.
8. Displaying your widget collection.
9. Expanding your widget collection.
10. Widgets for profit.

That begins to look quite reasonable. You need to be able to write at least 4,000 words under each of those chapter headings to make a worthwhile book. The minimum for a non-fiction book is 35,000 words – 40,000 is a better target.

The synopsis

Now, you have to write the synopsis. This outlines what you will write under each of the chapter headings. Clearly you must really know your subject to write the synopsis.

You should aim at writing, in almost note form, 70 to 80 words about each chapter content. Thus:

4 John Smith – widget-maker

Born 1803, Wakefield, of craftsman family. Primary schooling only. After school, trained, then worked, as corn dolly maker. In spare time, whittled. Seen at this, by champion Yorkshire whittler Albert Ramble, who thereafter trained him well. Later, was given a Yugoslavian widget and copied it. Demand grew.

So did his skill. J Smith greatly improved widget design and even found new uses for them. 1883, appointed Widget-maker Royal. J Smith widgets very rare collectors' items.

Write like this on each of the chapters in the book. While writing the synopsis, think whether you will be able to expand each chapter to the necessary minimum of 4,000 words. Think of it in roughly 50-word sections. Can you write 500 words about John Smith's early life, before he left school? And will it be of interest?

You may need to revise your thinking as you write the synopsis. Maybe one topic will make two chapters and another be better tagged on the end of another chapter. Retain a flexible approach. Satisfy yourself that you can produce nine or ten chapters, adding up to a roughly 40,000-word book that will interest budding widget collectors.

The accompanying statement

The synopsis done, you now need an accompanying statement. This will include a brief description of the book's objective, an explanation of why you are the ideal writer of the book, and an assessment of the market – the need and the competition – for the book.

All that initial research now comes into its own. Don't hide your light under any bushels: be positive and ... pushy. Sell yourself and the idea for the book.

You are the best writer in the country to write a book such as you propose. You have already written articles about widgets (enclose one perhaps) and you have already had a book published about your collection of dustbin lids. At the collector level, you know more about widgets than anyone else. (And you possess the biggest and best collection.) Your book will be better than its competitors – for the reasons we discussed earlier. You believe that there is a big, untapped demand for such a book.

Put all that in a carefully thought-out 400-word, close-typed single-sheet assessment/statement. A lot will depend on it. You have got to grab the publisher's attention with that page; the synopsis is of almost secondary importance.

Which publisher?

Now, at last, you are ready to go. You will already have given some thought to the most appropriate publisher. Who has similar books in an ongoing series, but lacks one on widgets? Who published the out-of-date books you uncovered? Do you think the publisher of one of the 'recent' books would be interested in one with a different approach? Who published your book on dustbin lids – a fairly 'off-the-wall' subject – and might they be interested in widgets too? What about other 'craft' book publishers?

List the likely publishers – realistically, there won't be many for a specialist book – in order of preference. (Most of the mainstream publishers are listed in the two annuals: the *Writers' and Artists' Yearbook* and *The Writer's Handbook* mentioned on page 50.)

Write – briefly – to the first on your list of likely publishers. Though it is becoming more common to write to more than one publisher with such a query; I prefer to approach one at a time, even if it does mean waiting. Say just that you are proposing to write a book about widgets and that you enclose a brief synopsis and assessment of the objectives and market for the book. Ask if they would be interested in such a book. Enclose a stamped addressed envelope and wait.

I believe that most British publishers prefer a 'hard copy' approach like that to an email query.

Sample chapters

While you are waiting, get on with producing a couple of chapters. Don't write more than two chapters until you get a firm contract from the publisher. (We'll look briefly at publishers' contracts in the next chapter.) But most publishers will want to see samples before they give you a contract.

It won't matter to the publisher which ones you offer as

samples but if possible I suggest you avoid Chapter 1. Chapter 1 in a non-fiction book is often an introductory chapter: it is therefore perhaps best written last, when you know what you have to introduce. It is the first thing bookshop browsers will glance at – it has to interest them quickly. It needs a lot of work, particularly on the first page – the 'hook'.

The choice of sample chapters is important. If possible, tell the publisher that you have sample chapters X and Y available. And make sure you get them complete and ready before the publisher has time to reply to your query. If you don't specify which chapters are ready, he may ask for chapters on aspects of the subject you know least about, and still need to brush up your research on.

Because the sample chapters are what your whole book will be judged on, make them extra good. If your book is to have illustrations (and illustrations are important to many non-fiction books) then provide illustrations with the samples. Provide all relevant tables, examples, summaries, too. These initial chapters should be a near-exact sample of what the finished book will be. Subject, of course, to your amending them if necessary (e.g. for consistency) as you write the rest of the book.

Publishers' changes

Publishers will sometimes ask you to make changes to the synopsis of your book. There are good reasons for such requests.

They may want your book to fit into the standard format of an ongoing series. This is very much to your advantage: series of non-fiction books tend to sell better than one-off 'stand-alone' titles. Or they may judge your coverage incomplete or excessive. They may even ask you to vary your writing style – for a different readership, perhaps.

Nine times out of ten – or even 99 times out of 100 – you should comply with the publishers' requests. Authors of non-fiction instructional or 'encyclopaedic' books cannot afford to be *prima donnas*. Publishers know the market into which your book will sell. They know what makes a book sell. That's their job. Your job is to write the best book you can.

After the go-ahead

Eventually – not necessarily with the first publisher you try – you will reach agreement on your proposed book. The publisher will give you the go-ahead and prepare a contract. Now, all you've got to do is write the book. And, don't forget, you are now *committed* to writing it. The publisher may pay you an advance against the royalties (see the next chapter); you have to earn it. You are also committed to a length and a delivery date – these too you must comply with, see below.

Novelists sometimes get stuck with their books; they can't think what to write next, how to get their heroine out of a corner they have written her into. This – and similar manifestations – is known as *writer's block*.

A non-fiction author should not suffer from writer's block – at least not in mid-book. You know what to write next; your synopsis lists every major topic you are intending to cover. And, a bonus: if you can't find the right words for one topic, write about a different one. You can always slot in the difficult, passed-over topic later.

Getting down to it

You have already organised your book into chapters. For each chapter the agreed synopsis will have eight to ten items listed in it. Now all you've got to do is write it.

Aim at writing about 500 words on each topic listed in the synopsis. (There's nothing rigid about that number of words though, it's merely a guideline.) Provided you know your subject, 500 words are easy to write. You are not faced with the perhaps daunting prospect of writing 4,000 to 5,000 words about anything. The book is broken down into manageable, 'non-frightening-sized' bites.

However you structure it, you are now launched into the actual writing. When you think you've finished writing your book though, you've still got a way to go. Just as with fiction, a good non-fiction book is not just written, it's rewritten. You need to review your work and polish it. Watch out for repetition, for inconsistencies, for less-than-perfect 'flow'. Turn the first draft into an easy-to-read useful book. Work at it. It will pay off.

The word budget

As already mentioned, when you sign up for a non-fiction book, you commit yourself to a finished length. Your publisher will have determined that, at that length, your book makes financial sense. You must not now write a significantly shorter or longer book.

You can keep a check on the length of your book as you write it, by using what I call a 'word budget'. Fig. 6 shows the word budget for this book – and how my predicted chapter-lengths varied as I wrote.

Suppose the contract is for a 40,000-word book in ten chapters. Simplistically, that is 4,000 words per chapter. But when you review the accepted synopsis in greater detail, you decide that some chapters ought to be longer, and some shorter. Or maybe you decide to divide one chapter into two. So long as the revised lengths still add up to about 40,000 words, this doesn't matter. If not, think again.

Before you start to write, list the chapters and, alongside, note their likely, or target, length. Your synopsis lists eight topics to cover in, say, Chapter 2. (I prefer to write Chapter 1 later.) You expect to write about 500 words on each. Target: 4,000 words. You complete the chapter. The word count is only 3,200 words. At this rate the book will be twenty per cent short. This would probably not be acceptable.

Review the synopsis and your initial word budget. Can you write more in each of the remaining chapters to make up the Chapter 2 shortfall? At this early stage, your view is probably that you can. Press on.

'HOBBY' WORD BUDGET AND PROGRESS				
Chapter	Target words	Running target	Achieved words	Achieved total
1	3,000	3,000	2,800	2,800
2	2,000	5,000	2,200	5,000
3	4,000	9,000	3,800	8,800
4	2,000	11,000	2,000	10,800
5	3,000	14,000	3,600	14,400
6	3,500	17,500	4,100	18,500
7	4,000	21,500	4,500	23,000
8	5,000	26,500	4,700	27,700
9	3,500	30,000	2,900	30,600
10	4,500	34,500	4,200	34,800
11	4,500	39,000	3,700	38,500
12	1,000	40,000	1,000	39,500
Appdx			500	40,000
Illns:say=	2,000		2,000	42,000

Fig. 6. Complete example of a combined word budget and record of progress – for this book. (I hadn't originally accounted for the illustrations, but was 'allowed' 7.5% 'leeway' on the 40,000-word total.)

Now write Chapter 3. If it *over*-runs the budget, you are probably all right. But if this one also turns out shorter than the budget, you may be in trouble. You need to review your whole schedule and approach.

Are your explanations simple and sufficient? Are your descriptions clear and colourful? Or are you perhaps assuming too much existing knowledge on the part of the reader? Can you incorporate some (or more) examples?

And so you progress through the book, matching output against word budget. That way, your book ends up the 'right' length. Ignoring your word budget can lead to disaster. A 40,000-word book may be financially viable; a 30,000- or 90,000-word book could well not be.

Working to time

You must also monitor your progress towards the delivery date. I usually plan to write a comfortable minimum 800 words per writing day – a 'standard' chapter a week. My delivery date agreement is based on this assumption. I keep a close check on my daily and weekly out-turn. If I am falling behind, I work longer hours. I always strive to complete ahead of schedule – and usually succeed.

Publishers have production schedules for all their new books; they have to book a 'time-slot' for their editors, and at the printers. Authors are required to deliver their work on time, to fit into this production schedule. That's the theory – the practice sometimes differs.

Your publisher's problems are not your concern. You should always strive to deliver on, or ahead of, time. Production delays are not then your fault. If you do hold up the production staff by late delivery though, it is possible that you could be held responsible for the cost of the delays.

Chapter 11:

Professionalism

Your writing is your hobby, not your profession. But the underlying principle of this book is that it is The Hobby That Pays. And to get paid, you must *act professionally*.

The more professional your work looks, the better chance you have of selling it. A scruffy-looking, badly-set-out piece of work is not likely to commend itself to the editor's immediate attention.

Your work, as it arrives on an editorial or publishing desk has to stand on its own two feet. You will not be there to make a sales pitch on its behalf. Your work is its own shop-window. Make it look good.

Presentation

You have finished writing your short story, article, novel or non-fiction book. You have 'polished' the words to a glistening shine. You can do no more to improve it.

For submission to an editor or publisher, your work must be typed. With the possible exception of paid 'Letters to the Editor' – and even these can usefully be typed, like any letter – or *children's* submissions to children's magazines, any submission which is not typed will most likely not be considered at all. Almost certainly, it will be consigned straight to the waste-bin. No one has the time, or the inclination, to try to interpret a writer's handwriting.

So your manuscript must be typed. Let's take it for granted that you are using a computer/word processor. Word processor programs offer you the choice of many fonts in many sizes.

For the preparation of a typescript for submission to a magazine or publishing house, you must choose a 'conventional' font, not one of the fancy imitation-joined-up-handwriting ones. Go for Arial or Times New Roman or similar. And a font size of around 11 or 12. My own preference for all purposes is 11-point Tahoma – it's a nice 'clean' typeface, without serifs. (See Fig. 7.)

Your work must be typed/printed on white A4 paper which should not be too thick nor too thin. Thick paper will push up any postage costs, and is unnecessary; thin paper is flimsy and looks mean. An 80 gsm paper – as used in photocopiers – is about right. Some amateurs submit their work on coloured paper in the hope that it will 'stand out'. It does: it gets rejected quicker. Stick to white paper.

Your work must be presented double-spaced. That means type a line, miss a line, type a line, etc. Your word processor will do it for you – just click on format, paragraph and double-spacing.

Margins

The printed typescript must have large margins all round. Allow a wide left margin – 1.5 to 2 inches – and about an inch at top, bottom and right.

Your word processor is capable of *right-justifying* your typescript. Right-justified typescript has a neatly aligned right edge – just like in a printed book. Editors, publishers and typesetters alike all prefer to work from *unjustified* typescript, that is, with the old-fashioned ragged right edge. The reason for this preference is that computerised right-justification fills the line, from margin to margin, by adding spaces between words. Then no one knows for sure whether a double space is the writer's intention, or an automatic computer insert. So don't right-justify.

Page numbering

Obviously, you will number the pages of your typescript. Go further: identify each page as part of a specific article, story or

Subheads/Wells/1

SUBHEADS AND SIDEBARS

Gordon Wells

Short stories often look more attractive – an easier read – than feature articles. Apart from a perhaps tempting title and an interesting illustration, this is partly due to the amount of 'white space' on the pages.

White space

Cast your mind back to those replica copies of hundred-year-old newspapers: every page a solid boring grey unleavened by illustrations or splash headlines. Compare that image with today's broadsheets – let alone the tabloids. Nowadays, newspapers look less off-putting, more readable, with illustrations and large headlines within their own ample white space. And it is that white space that, in part, makes the pages look welcoming and attractive.

Back now to short stories and articles. The dialogue in most short stories generates many short paragraphs, with opening indents and frequent half-line ends – all of which mean white space … and give the appearance of an 'easy read'.

Let's look at how the non-fiction writer can apply those same principles.

Subheads/Wells/5

lengths but to go with the typical feature t right. And of course, there's nothing to your article. The word 'offering' is ial part of the article – if it is, incorporate always be an optional extra for the editor's decision. (Make it good and the editor will usually find room for it.)

Even more than any other part of a feature article, the sidebar should be well-organised and easy to assimilate. Bullet-pointed items are a particularly good way of listing the material. (And, as evidenced above, a bullet-pointed list is always a Good Thing in a feature article – it generates white space (see above) and is 'easy to read'.)

Sidebars, as such, are seldom appropriate in a non-fiction book but, occasionally in 'the right sort of book', a piece of information can be boxed – to give it added importance. And of course, there are always chapter-end summaries which serve a not-too-dissimilar function in more technical books.

Overall, subheads and sidebars improve the appearance of and enhance the readability of much non-fiction. They are useful tools.

                END   1000 words   [12subhead]

Gordon Wells, address
<email address>
telephone number

Fig. 7. The first and last pages of the typescript of a feature article, showing layout – margins, double-spaced text, header, title, etc.

book. This helps to reinstate a complete document when, for instance, the pages fall on the floor.

When preparing a book manuscript – either fiction or non-fiction – number the book pages straight through. Do not – as you might in a technical report, say – number the pages in each chapter separately. The preliminary pages in a book manuscript though – see later in this chapter – should always be numbered separately.

It is common practice to identify and number pages in the top right corner. There's nothing wrong with identifying at the top and numbering at the foot of the page, but both together at top right is more conventional. Type something like Title/Wells/3 at top right and then continue the type-script two or three lines further down. This identifying and numbering is known as a header – the word processor will set it up for you, automatically.

Paragraph layout

Indent your paragraphs, uniformly, usually by half an inch. Ideally (but not a major point) don't indent the first paragraph of an article, short story or book chapter. Nor the first paragraph beneath a sub-head. (Notice this book's layout.)

Do not – as you might in a business letter – leave a blank line between paragraphs. If your article or non-fiction book has sub-headings though, leave a blank line above and below the heading. Similarly, in technical articles or non-fiction books, if you use bullet points or similar, leave a blank line above and below the list.

First and last pages

The first page of an article, or short story, or book chapter should each be similarly set out. Scroll down a few lines and, if appropriate, type the chapter number; scroll down a few more lines and type the article, story or chapter title, but don't underline it. For articles and short stories, scroll down a couple more lines and type your name or pen-name; scroll down two or three more lines and start the text.

Continue typing your article or short story to its end. Then, immediately below the last line of text, type a row of dots and the word END – so that the typesetter knows he's finished. At the end of a book chapter, just type the dots, not the END, until the last chapter.

Again, for a short story or article, you need to give your name (real and 'pen') and address – nowadays, your email address and phone number are useful too – at the end of the typescript. I type the postal address in a single line across the page, the email address and phone number are on the next two lines, centred. For a book, I add a final page – after END – with just my name and address, etc. centred on it.

Fig. 7 shows how the first and last pages of a stand-alone typescript should be laid out.

When you have finished printing out your immaculate-looking word-processed pages, you should read them through again. Inevitably you will find at least one overlooked typing error. Correct it on your computer file and reprint that page.

A cover page

There are two schools of thought about article/short story cover pages: one school says provide them, the other says don't. I belong to the school that provides cover pages . . . when submitting work by post. I think it makes the work look more professional. But, of course, increasingly articles and short stories are being submitted to editors as email attachments, in which case I don't bother with the cover page. I would not recommend article and short story submission by email for the first 'attack' on a new market – unless you already know that the editor actively prefers submission in that form. Until you know the market, I would submit initially by post.

A cover page has no header; a third to half-way down the page, type the title of the piece. Two or three lines below that, type your name (or pen-name if using one); a few more lines below that, type 'Approximately 000 words on 00 sheets of typescript' (and, if appropriate, 'accompanied by 00 black and white/colour photographs by the writer.'). Scroll down to near the page foot and type your name (again, real and 'pen') and address details in the lower left corner. If for a short story, add in, at top right corner, the rights on offer. FBSR (see below) is assumed for articles and doesn't need to be specified.

If you don't provide a cover page then all the relevant information should be either at the top of page 1 or at the end of the work. With email submissions, I specify the number of words on the 'END' line.

Preliminary pages of books (prelims)

Now let's leave articles and short stories for a moment and think about book presentation. Look at almost any book. Only the cheapest of pulp novels starts the story on the first page. More usually, there are several pages in front of the text giving the book title, copyright notice, list of contents, etc. These are known as the book's preliminary pages – the *prelims*. For hardback books there is a fairly standard format for the prelims:

- The half-title – just the book title, always a right-hand (*recto*) page. In paperback books this page is sometimes used for an extract from, or a blurb about, the book.
- The half-title *verso* – the back of the half-title, always a left-hand (*verso*) page. Sometimes left blank, sometimes used to list related books.
- The title-page – always a right-hand page, contains the book title, the author's name and the publisher's name/ imprint.
- The title-page *verso* – the back of the title-page, always a left-hand page, contains essential legal and bibliographical material. The author's copyright notice, the date(s) of publication, maybe the ISBN – International Standard Book Number, which is added by the publisher later – and the names of relevant artists, printers, etc.
- The contents page(s) – conventionally, a right-hand page. The first page of text is also conventionally a right-hand

page, which may entail leaving a blank page vi, or it may be used for a list of illustrations or acknowledgements.

If a dedication is required, this should be included at the outset and will need a page as well.

There is nothing sacrosanct about the prelims. It is not at all unusual for the publishers of paperback books to cut them back – perhaps omitting pages i and ii above. And with novels, there is less justification for page v. The only real essentials – for both publisher and author – are the 'legal' title-page and title-page verso.

A conscientious non-fiction book author though, should provide draft typescript for the full set of prelims. The publisher will appreciate this thoughtfulness – and can discard any pages not required. A novelist, though, will seldom provide more than the title page.

Submitting articles and stories to editors

In the previous chapter we looked at the way in which a publisher should be approached about a non-fiction book. Articles and short stories, going to magazine editors, need a different treatment.

I have already mentioned (in Chapter 6) the increasing demand for advance outlines for articles – submitted as a query to editors before working up and submitting the full article. These apart, there are some occasions when a completed manuscript is to be submitted *on spec*. I have also discussed the advantages of not aiming too high with early submissions. Although many magazines either say, 'no unsolicited submissions' or, 'enclose samples of similar published work', there are still some, at the lower-paying end of the market, who will look at unsolicited feature articles and short stories. And, because you have done your market research, you think it likely that . . . *Peg's Paper*, say, will be interested in your work.

At this early stage in your writing career, I recommend submitting your complete *on spec* story or article by post. Even if you live next door to the editorial offices, post it, or at least deliver it in a sealed envelope, through the letter-box. Do not try to deliver by hand, direct to the editor.

Covering letters to editors

When delivering by post, it is best to enclose a covering letter. Find out the name of the Editor, or Features Editor, or Fiction Editor, either from the magazine's masthead page, or by phoning and asking the receptionist or switchboard operator. Address the appropriate person by name.

Your covering letter should say little more than:

The Features Editor
Peg's Paper

Dear Jane Smith

I enclose herewith, for your consideration [making clear it's *on spec*] for publication at your normal rates of payment [i.e. you expect to be paid – it's not a freebie] a 000-word article [i.e. fact, not fiction, and the right length] about beekeeping, entitled [identification] 'How D'you Tell One Bee from Another?'

I have kept bees for the last twenty years [i.e. your 'credentials'] and feel that my experiences will interest your many rural-based readers [showing that you have studied the magazine and its readership].

If the article is not of interest to you, I would appreciate its return. I enclose a stamped addressed envelope. [Without this, your submission is likely to go straight to the waste-bin.]

I look forward to hearing from you.

Yours sincerely

Keeping tabs on submissions

As soon as you have submitted an article or short story to an editor, forget it. Get on with researching and writing the next one. If you don't keep at it, you'll never progress.

But you also need to keep tabs on what you've submitted where and when. If you don't get a reply from a magazine within about five or six weeks, you can reasonably send the editor a gentle reminder-cum-query. And if, as you should, you have been busying yourself with other articles and stories in the meantime, you won't remember when you submitted it. So keep simple records.

It is best to start with a system that will cope with your output as it grows. I keep my records on the computer in the form of a table. The column headings are:

- Article/story number – I number sequentially within each year.
- Filename – all work is saved on the computer – the filenames help locate them.
- Title – in case the filename is very different, the actual title, abbreviated.
- Words/pictures – 1200/2 means a 1,200-word article with two illustrations.
- To – name of magazine.
- Date submitted.
- Accept/Reject. (A for accept, R for reject.)
- Decision date – gives a useful 'feel' for later reference.
- Date published – which will affect payment date.
- Paid – amount.
- Date paid.

Depending on the last column with an entry in it, I know whether to chase for decision, publication date or payment. The system works for me.

Rights

Beginners often worry about *Rights*. Don't. As soon as you commit your work to paper or computer memory it is your copyright. You can do with it what you will.

When you offer an article or story to a UK magazine you will usually be offering First British Serial Rights (FBSR) in it. 'Serial rights' means in a magazine or other 'serial' publication. 'First British' means what it says – its first publication in Britain. And you are offering the 'Right' to publish.

FBSR is important to short story writers. They can sometimes sell Second Rights, or First Scandinavian Rights in the unchanged story. There is, though, virtually no market for Second Rights in an article – articles are written in the style of the magazine targeted.

I will relinquish virtually any Rights in an article – because I can rewrite the article in a slightly different way and offer First Rights again. I have written several articles about dragons: many of the facts are common to all the articles, but I have used them in different ways – mixed and matched them. Selling several articles from one piece of research is being professional.

Remember: there is no copyright in facts, nor in ideas, nor in titles. The copyright is only in the way the facts are written about, the way you string the words together.

Selling a novel

I have explained how to offer short stories and articles to magazines; I have explained how you should go about selling your non-fiction book before you write it. What about your novel? How are you going to sell that?

First, you cannot, as a beginner, realistically expect to sell your novel before you finish writing it, whereas even a beginner can expect to sell a non-fiction book from the synopsis, etc. Secondly, many publishers prefer receiving work only through an agent – and agents are as hard to find as publishers. See below.

There are, however, some publishers who will consider first novels. And undoubtedly some first novels get accepted and published. To repeat, your chances will be better if your novel is in a specific genre.

A possible approach to a publisher is:

1. Identify a publisher who publishes work similar to your own – and don't think only of the major publishing houses, a smaller firm may well be a better bet.
2. Identify the relevant editor at that publishing house (phone and ask the operator, as for magazines).
3. Check – on the Internet – whether the publisher will look at submitted work and has a standard form in which they prefer work to be submitted. Most often, if they will look at submissions at all, they will require a detailed synopsis plus the first three chapters.
4. Submit the material, as specified, direct to the chosen editor with a covering letter. Enclose a suitable envelope and sufficient stamps (or a cheque) to cover return postage. It's a good idea to ask for an acknowledgment of receipt – one way is to enclose a stamped and pre-printed card, saying merely that [Title] has been received by [Publisher] on [Date]. You may well have to wait up to three months for the publisher's decision, especially if your submission is being seriously considered.

And because it is hard to find an agent to take on a beginner, it is worth approaching agents at the same time as publishers, in a parallel campaign. Adopt much the same procedure as outlined above.

Agents

Agents are what their name says: they are people who act on behalf of their clients. They are skilled at negotiating with publishers – they know what the market will bear; they should be experienced editors of the type of work they handle; and they will often help/encourage their client-authors through bad literary patches – 'blocks', etc.

They know what sort of book which publisher is looking for. They will only offer a publisher work which is both up to standard and appropriate to that publisher's list. To the publisher, an agent is an excellent 'first filter', protecting him from the great mass of unacceptable material.

Agents make their living by acting for their clients. If they don't sell your work, they don't get paid; their pay is a set percentage (usually 10 to 15 per cent) of your earnings as a writer. And of course, the corollary of that is that an agent won't take you on if he or she doesn't think you are likely to earn enough money to be worth the time spent agenting you.

You can succeed without an agent, though. You will not need – or be able to get – an agent for articles or short stories. I believe that a non-fiction author should be able to manage perfectly well on careful market study in lieu of an agent. For many years now, I have not had an agent for my non-fiction books, and have sold them all without too much difficulty. It is for full-length fiction that an agent is most desirable. Even there, there are plenty of successful authors who work un-agented. Without an agent, you just need to be a better business-person and study the market yourself.

Book contracts

Whether you have written a novel or a non-fiction book, once you succeed in selling it, you will receive a contract – an Agreement. And even if you have an agent you would be wise to know a little about this document. (I can only touch the high spots in this section of this book: a whole book could be written about publishers' contracts.)

A book contract is a (fairly) standard document. Publishers don't like making changes to them, but they will. But what are the agreements really about? You, the author, agree to provide (or have already provided) a book of a certain length by no later than an agreed date. You will discuss the length and delivery date with the publisher and agree them. You must then adhere to them. You certify that your book is original and not libellous.

The publisher in turn agrees to publish your book within a reasonable time (not always clearly specified); the publisher usually agrees to pay you royalties (an amount of money per copy sold); the publisher often agrees to pay you a non-returnable advance against future royalties. The advance could well be returnable if you don't deliver the promised book – the 'non-returnable' relates to sales not coming up to expectations.

There are two ways of determining royalties. Royalties have long been based on a percentage of the list (or cover) price of the book. For hardback books, the royalty rate is often 10 per cent; for paperbacks, between 5 and 8 per cent – the lower rate for mass-market sales. Increasingly, royalty rates today are based on the publisher's net receipts from sales of the book. The publisher sells the book to bookshops at a discount – anything from 40 to 60 per cent. The author gets his percentage royalty based on the less-than-full-price figure.

To illustrate: a 'list-price' royalty of 8 per cent on a £10 paperback book means the author gets 80 pence per book sold. An 8 per cent 'net receipts' royalty on the same book sold at a 50 per cent discount to a big chain bookseller, would earn the author only 40 pence. Clearly, the author should expect a 'net receipts' royalty rate to be about twice that for a 'list-price' royalty.

An advance can be paid in one, two or three tranches: on signature of contract, on delivery (and acceptance) of manuscript, and on publication of the book. It's the same amount of money, in one, two or three bites.

A now old-fashioned rule of thumb for the likely size of an advance is that it represents the royalty earnings from the sale of half the first print run. Take a hardback novel to sell at £15, with 10 per cent list-price royalty. The first print run for a hardback first novel might be 2,000 copies. The advance could then be:

$$2000 \times 0.5 \times £15 \times 0.1 = £1,500.$$

No further royalties would be paid until the advance had been 'earned out' – i.e. until 1,000 copies had been sold.

Chapter 12:

A Writer's Life

Writing is a solitary hobby. Nobody can hold your hand as you gaze at the blank computer screen or the unblemished sheet of paper. Well, not to any literary purpose, anyway.

It can also be a lonely hobby. Novelists, of course, populate their world with self-created characters – and are therefore never really alone. Short story characters, though, have a shorter shelf-life; and the unfortunate writer of non-fiction – books or articles – must research and write all alone.

But don't let this put you off. If you were going to be put off, you would never have reached this final chapter. The writing itself should be, and often is, so engrossing that you never notice the loneliness.

For the first dozen or so years of my 'writing career', I don't recall ever meeting another writer. To friends and relations I was just slightly unusual: I preferred writing to sailing or playing golf. This didn't strike me as strange.

Then one weekend, I went to a writers' conference and the world changed. There were lots of people just like me and many were far more accomplished. I had a lot to learn. But I was no longer alone. And I discovered that there were writers' clubs, other, bigger, writing conferences and get-togethers, books about writing, and magazines too. Since then, I've never looked back. Many of my best friends are writers and I've steadily pulled myself up to somewhere nearer to their writing standard.

Wherever you live, at least some of these contacts are available to you. I just didn't know. As a beginner, there is much to be gained from involvement with other writers.

Writing clubs, classes and conferences

Ask at your local library or bookshop; there may be a writers' club – or 'writers' circle' as they are often called – near you; the library or bookshop should know. If there is one, check it out.

Check out your local schools, adult education departments, colleges and universities too: many offer evening classes or one-day weekend courses in writing subjects.

Such evening classes are often in 'Creative Writing' – a title which slightly worries me. My view is that you should always write with the thought of paid publication in mind; the requirements of the market-place should influence your work.

'Creative writing', though, is sometimes seen as a purely artistic exercise, or undertaken for therapeutic reasons. There's nothing wrong with that approach, as such, but the real purpose of writing requires there to be a reader – preferably many readers – and that means publication.

Certainly, as a beginner, you should get a lot of useful help and support from almost any group of writers; you have much to learn. Many writing clubs/circles concentrate on everyone reading their work aloud for other members to criticize. Listen carefully to the criticisms – but decide for yourself whether or not to accept them. Beware 'the blind leading the blind'. It is well worth quietly investigating the 'credentials' of your critics – have they achieved mainstream publication themselves? If not, is their advice of value?

Bigger writing conferences are usually of greater value. Most offer a number of formal talks by big-name writers; we can all learn from these. Many conferences also incorporate short courses, discussion groups and/or workshops; these can be particularly helpful. They are usually led by writers well-experienced in their particular field. Criticism or advice by such writers will be far more valuable than that from even the best-intentioned fellow-strugglers. If you hear of a conference being held near you, do enrol.

The biggest – and by far the best – writers' conference in Britain is Swanwick: The Writers' Summer School. Attended by up to 300 writers – from absolute beginners to best-sellers – 'Swanwick', as it is known, is a week-long event. It has been held at The Hayes Conference Centre, Swanwick, Derbyshire every August since 1949. Writers come regularly from as far afield as America, Africa and Israel to 'recharge their batteries' and renew friendships. Each year there are big-name speakers, a wide choice of four-lecture courses and two-session workshops and lots of one-off talks; there's plenty of social life too. Details are on the school's website: *www.wss.org.uk*.

Another regular, but smaller, writers' get-together is The Southern Writers' Conference (*www.southernwriters.co.uk*). There are also many one-day events at various venues all over the country. Watch out for one near you.

Writing magazines

There are other ways of keeping in touch with what's going on in the writing world. There are some excellent writing magazines, not only British but also two important American ones.

The main British magazines are:

Writers' News, monthly – website *www.writersnews.co.uk* – which is available on subscription only, and its sister publication . . .
Writing Magazine, monthly – same website as *Writers' News* – available on subscription and from newsagents.
Writers' Forum, monthly – website *www.writers-forum.com* – which is available on subscription and from newsagents.
The New Writer, bi-monthly – website *www.thenewwriter.com* – available on subscription only.

And the two leading US writers' magazines are:

Writer's Digest, monthly – website *www.writersdigest.com*, and
The Writer, monthly – website *www.writermag.com*.

Books about writing

Not really a means of getting together, but of immense value to all beginning writers, there are also books about writing. Any book on a specific writing field will take you further than has been possible within the confines of this general introduction.

Appendix:

Ideas for Ideas

As already mentioned, every writer needs a steady supply of ideas – for the next short story or article, for the next book. Some writers seem to have a never-ending flood of ideas: the rest of us have to work at developing them.

Here are 20 ready-made ideas for ideas:

1. Investigate the current 'Top 20' pop songs. Turn a song into a storyline. Even a title can spark off ideas.
2. Search the 'agony columns' for ideas for short stories and articles. These are real people's problems – and good for stories or advice articles.
3. Investigate local history (maybe on the gravestones) for potential saga plots.
4. List your own interests and expertise. Cross-match them. I photograph statues and am interested in English revolutions/uprisings. I sold two articles on London's statues of revolutionaries.
5. List 10, 12, or 20 'tips' (7 or 13 tips don't 'sound right'), or an ABC – on almost anything you know about.
6. Take the 'blurb' of a published short story, which you then don't read. Write your own story to fit the blurb. It will be different from the unread published one.
7. Listen to other people's conversations. Put your own speculative background to overheard remarks.
8. Capitalise on your own personal experiences.
9. Collect newspaper cuttings about anything unusual – then group them together for an 'unusual' article.
10. Don't avoid your research digressions – be led astray. Today's side-track may be tomorrow's feature.

11. Remember (and ask yourself) the six 'Kipling questions' – Who? What? Why? Where? When? How? – about almost anything. The answers can lead to an interesting feature article.

12. Collect pictures of interesting-looking men and women. In a spare moment, invent a dossier on each of them. Use that in a future story.

13. Listen to friends' tales of unusual experiences. Write them up, maintaining the friends' anonymity.

14. Sit back and observe the passing scene – in bus, train, or park. Ask yourself, 'What if . . .?' about your unwitting companions.

15. Pick a word at random from a dictionary. Develop the theme of a story or article from that word.

16. Open your mind to catch chance thoughts and ideas – they're all about us. But make a note of any passing ideas you catch – otherwise, they escape again.

17. Watch out for any 'interesting' characters – the bag lady, the harassed mum, the lonely Colonel Blimp. Write an imaginary dossier about them. Then play 'What if . . .?'

18. Take a familiar nursery rhyme or bedtime story and update it. The three little pigs might become present-day youngsters of widely different means, coping with a property developer 'wolf'.

19. Choose two or three of your friends who don't know each other. Write a description of each, with new names. Then invent a situation where they might meet and have to cope with some conflict situation. The makings of a storyline.

20. Take one of your rejected stories. Rewrite it from a different viewpoint. Take an old article and rewrite it for a new market. Never sell an article just once.

Index